© Luca Pioltelli

About the Authors

CAITLIN FRIEDMAN, the original cofounder of the boutique public relations agency YC Media with Kimberly Yorio, is now a full-time writer and consultant living in Brooklyn, New York.

KIMBERLY YORIO is the president of YC Media, specializing in publicity for cookbooks, restaurants, wine and spirits, food products, and media training. Kim lives in Weehawken, New Jersey.

They are the coauthors of four books, including *The Girl's Guide to Being a Boss*; *The Girl's Guide to Big Bold Career Success*; and *Happy at Work, Happy at Home*.

the girl's guide to starting your own business

*Candid Advice, Frank Talk,
and True Stories for
the Successful Entrepreneur*

Caitlin Friedman & Kimberly Yorio

REVISED EDITION

HARPER
BUSINESS

HARPER

BUSINESS

A hardcover edition of this book was published in 2003, and a paperback edition was published in 2004, by Collins.

THE GIRL'S GUIDE TO STARTING YOUR OWN BUSINESS (REVISED EDITION). Copyright © 2003, 2010 by Caitlin Friedman and Kimberly Yorio. All rights reserved. Printed in the United States of America. No part of this book may be used or reproduced in any manner whatsoever without written permission except in the case of brief quotations embodied in critical articles and reviews. For information address HarperCollins Publishers Inc., 10 East 53rd Street, New York, NY 10022.

HarperCollins books may be purchased for educational, business, or sales promotional use. For information please write: Special Markets Department, HarperCollins Publishers Inc., 10 East 53rd Street, New York, NY 10022.

FIRST HARPER BUSINESS PAPERBACK REVISED EDITION PUBLISHED 2010.

Designed by Lee Fukui

The Library of Congress has catalogued the previous edition as follows:

Friedman, Caitlin.
    The girl's guide to starting your own business: candid advice, frank talk, and true stories for the successful entrepreneur / Caitlin Friedman and Kimberly Yorio.—1st ed.
        p.   cm.
    Includes index.
    ISBN 0-06-052157-0 (hc : acid-free paper)

    1. Women executives.   2. Businesswomen.   3. Self-employed.   4. Personnel management.   I. Yorio, Kimberly.   II. Title.

HD6054.3.F75 2003
658.1'1—dc21

2003059976

ISBN 978-0-06-198924-7 (pbk.)

13 14 OV 10 9 8 7 6 5 4 3 2

Contents

Acknowledgments   ix

Preface to the Revised Edition   xi

Introduction   1

1. Are You the Girl to Run the Show?   3

2. What Business Is Right for You?
   And the Baby Steps to Make It Happen   28

3. The Scary Stuff
   Legalities, Licenses, Permits, Financials, and Funding   49

4. Your Business Plan
   Why You Should Spend Your Precious Time Writing One   83

5. Sell It, Sister!
   Getting Your Name and Product "Out There"   100

6. Being a Boss Sucks
   But It Is Essential, and Often Satisfying   133

7. Acting Like an Adult
Finding Your Voice and Professional Style   164

8. The Girl's Guide to Surviving
Today's Technology   187

9. A Girl's Gotta Write
Proposals, Presentations, and Other Business Writing   205

10. It Couldn't Hurt
*Good Business Advice Your Grandmother
Would Have Given You (and Maybe Did)*   223

*Appendix: Helpful Web Sites for Girls
Going into Business*   245

Index   249

Acknowledgments

For this revised, updated, brand-spanking-new edition of *The Girl's Guide to Starting Your Own Business*, we wanted to thank Matthew Inman at HarperCollins, for believing the world needed it, and our agent, David Black, because he always has our backs.

We want to say a special thank-you to all of the girls who agreed to share their stories with us. A special thanks to our mothers (Joan and Sharyn) and Kim's sister (Kara) for their constant cheerleading.

Caitlin wants to thank Kim for being the best writing partner a girl could ask for.

And Kim wants to thank Caitlin for ten years of ideas, inspiration, and collaboration.

Preface to the Revised Edition

As the professional world becomes less dependable and jobs less traditional, many of us find ourselves on the brink of inevitable change. But counterintuitive as it may sound, these tumultuous times are exactly the time to follow your dream of becoming a small business owner and start on the path to a career that satisfies you professionally and emotionally. Taking control of your financial future is now, more than ever, the safer road. While it's been nearly ten years since we first wrote this book, our original goal for writing it hasn't changed: We want women to achieve their dreams of being a business owner and set their own terms for success. We want them to plan to embrace the bigger and better opportunities in the world.

When we started thinking about updating this book, we sat down and read it cover to cover. It had been awhile since we revisited the pages of our first girl's guide adventure, and we were pleasantly surprised by how much of the advice holds up. As fast as technology has advanced (Facebook and Twitter didn't exist when this book was first published) and the employment landscape has shifted (there wasn't an economic crisis when this was first published), the secrets to successful entrepreneurship remain the same. At the end of the day, a small business is about you. The way we sell, market, and fund our ventures may have changed, but the buck, and ultimately the success, still stops with you. Passion, drive, smarts, energy, a love of learning, a brilliant idea, an innovative process, a much-needed service—all come from you. So you had better create a business that will maximize the best and most successful aspects of you.

That said, even if the core of what makes an entrepreneur success-ful remains the same, many of the tools we have today that help us land funding, create marketing campaigns, and hire the best employees have changed. So, the reader eager to launch a business will find tips, advice, and stories throughout this updated version to help maximize the resources now available to us. We also went back to women we'd inter-viewed for the first book for updates, spoke to those on the cutting edge of workplace technology, and researched the most up-to-date statis-tics—all with the goal of arming those ready to take the leap.

As we were flipping through the chapters in this book and remi-niscing about the early days of our public relations business, YC Media, we also realized that we had no idea when we started out where the business would end up taking us. The process of launching, growing, shrinking, and reconfiguring our business has shaped us into the pro-fessionals and the women we are today. Our personal lives have also undergone radical changes as we started families; Kim got separated; and both of us added "author" to our lists of ways we define ourselves. What began as a public relations business has evolved into a collabora-tion that includes not only our PR business but a writing partnership that has yielded a series of four business books for women.

Through our ten-year journey, we accomplished a number of things we never expected. We overcame professional fears, such as public speaking, which enabled us to make appearances on national television and take part in speaking engagements with mentors and celebrities in front of thousands of people. We landed huge clients that were impressed enough with our presentations (moxie? nerve? chutzpah?) to take a chance on a tiny agency like ours. We met women all over the world through our travels and our web site who were inspired by our books. We received an award, made the *BusinessWeek* bestseller list twice, and wrote an article or two. We hired employees well and fired them poorly. We rode the profit and loss roller coaster as the national economy shifted (plummeted) below our feet. We also realized that after a decade of a successful partnership, we wanted different things and parted ways, leaving Kim happily spearheading the public relations busi-ness and Caitlin happily writing from home.

And we had no idea when we registered the business name that any of that was waiting for us.

So what's waiting for you in these pages?

A wild ride of your own. In this way, do what we say and do as we did—jump into it with both feet. Enjoy every second of picking a name, designing a logo, signing a lease, landing customers, and eventually, opening your doors.

We don't have a single regret. You won't either.

the girl's
guide to starting
your.own
business

Introduction

When we were in our late twenties and working as in-house publicists at two major New York publishing houses, we were tired. We were working days, nights, and weekends, then coming home to small, poorly furnished apartments, stacks of bills, and Ben-and-Jerry's-fueled daydreams of a better life.

Don't get us wrong, we loved our work. We were good at what we did, and we had a talent for it. People in the industry respected and trusted us. We were saddled with incredible responsibility: We created and managed budgets, supervised employees, and made a difference in our companies' revenues. We were each running a little company within a larger corporation. In other words, we were living the life of entrepreneurs but with none of the financial or spiritual perks.

It was time to make a change.

As we individually considered starting our own public relations businesses, we visited bookstores and conducted on-line searches to find information that would help us navigate the terrifying waters of self-employment. What we found were books that ranged from the vaguely helpful to the downright unreadable. We found books on marketing and books on funding, books on partnerships and books on parachutes. We found a lot of books about how to sound like a man and think like a man. But who wants to do *that*?

What we never found was the book that said, "You can do it, girl! All you need is _____, _____, and _____!" This book will fill in the blanks. And there are a lot of blanks.

The Girl's Guide to Starting Your Own Business is the book that we yearned for when we were starting our own respective businesses, and then when we merged them into one company. It addresses the unique challenges that women face (for example, finding female business role models, balancing family and work, being a boss without being a bitch) but also the power that our gender's distinct style and strengths bring to business. We encourage women to be women, especially in the business world.

While *The Girl's Guide to Starting Your Own Business* faces the fear factor of doing business as a woman head-on, it also delves into the countless opportunities for personal growth that can and should make the endeavor joyful. We have learned firsthand that if you have the right attitude, ideas, and talent, business can be fun. Choosing a logo, opening your company bank account, getting a corporate charge card, handing out your business card, and distributing a press release are all EXCITING steps in the process. And did we mention how great it feels to win your first account, make your first sale, or sign your first client? Or the incredible feeling of empowerment that comes with having the keys to your own office and walking into it each morning?

The Girl's Guide to Starting Your Own Business is for anyone who has a great business concept and is toying with the idea of going out on her own and prefers to be her own boss. This book is for anyone who needs to know where to start. And last, but certainly not least, *The Girl's Guide to Starting Your Own Business* is for potential entrepreneurs ready to flaunt their girlie-selves on their way to making their dreams come true.

Are You the Girl to Run the Show?

Stand up and walk to the nearest mirror. Take a long, hard look at the woman you see there. Now ask yourself, "Can I look to this woman for all the support, security, and leadership I need to survive?" Then ask that person in the mirror, "Do you *want* to be responsible for all the support, security, and leadership that I, the person holding the book, need?"

This chapter will help you evaluate whether you have what it takes to build your own business. Just as important, it will help you determine whether you really want to. You may fantasize about greeting customers in your own store or selling your hand-knit sweaters on-line, but after some exploration, you might discover that when it comes to the demands of minding a store, you would actually prefer to work a nine-to-five day and let someone else deal with the headaches of employees, leases, taxes, and contracts. Then again, you might decide that you are ready to take the leap.

So, let's take that long, hard look in the mirror, shall we?

The Good, Bad, and Unexpected Delights of Running the Show

We should point out at the start that nothing in business (like life) stays the same. Some days are good, some days are bad, and some are unexpectedly profitable, but tomorrow will always be different. While the basic joys of running the show stay the same, there are some days when you just need to remind yourself why you decided to start your own business.

The Good: What We Like About Running the Show

We think there are more good than bad things about starting a business. Adrienne Arieff, founder of Arieff Communications, a public relations business in San Francisco specializing in hotels and beauty products, offers this benefit to consider: "The good thing about running your own business is that the final decision is always yours to make."

These are some other benefits to running the show.

YOU ARE NEVER BORED. Those days of sitting at your desk, staring out the window fantasizing about running off with Jake Gyllenhaal are over. You now have work to do and the motivation to do it.

YOU WILL CONSTANTLY BE CHALLENGED. Let's say that you have a slow day (rare, we hope) and thoughts of Jake Gyllenhaal creep in, within the next minute or so, you will have an opportunity to create, execute, and manage something. It could be anything from working on a new window display to being interviewed about your business for an article in the local newspaper.

YOUR TIME IS YOUR OWN. It now benefits you, not someone else, to work harder and longer if need be. But if you have a doctor's appointment and are running a little late, that's fine, because now you have the most understanding boss in the world . . . YOU.

YOU HAVE THE OPPORTUNITY TO CREATE AN IDEAL WORK ENVIRONMENT. You can now create the work environment you have always been looking for in past jobs. Let's say you work best listening to a little Lady Gaga; you can do it, if you don't run a children's clothing store. Or, you prefer to start your day late and work until the wee hours. You can do it, if your business lends itself to those hours. Your company can be structured in ways that work best for you.

YOU DON'T HAVE TO EVER AGAIN BEG FOR A PROMOTION OR A RAISE FROM A BOSS. Okay, so you might have to ask for a fee increase from a client, but that is easier than begging for a salary bump from a supervisor who was passed out drunk at last year's holiday party. Need more money? With some careful planning and hard work, you can make it happen.

YOU CAN MAKE YOUR WORK FIT YOUR LIFE. For too long you have been squeezing in dates, doctor appointments, birthday celebrations, and your child's school play around your workday. Now you have the opportunity to create a career that fits your life. This isn't to say that you will work less (you will most likely be working more), but the timing of it is now up to you, and if getting to your child's play means locking up the office for an hour or two, so be it.

YOU DON'T HAVE A BOSS. We can't stress enough how GOOD this is. It is fantastic not to have anyone to answer to other than yourself (and sometimes investors, but we will get to that later). You now call the shots, set the agenda, make the schedule, hire and fire, reap the benefits and the profits of a successful endeavor. Nothing is better than that.

The Bad: What We Don't Like About Running the Show

It is important to remember that BAD should be temporary. If most of your day is spent worrying, stressing, obsessing, crying, or any *ing*'s other than *smiling* and *laughing*, then think about doing something else. Do expect some bad days, weeks, and months. As Adrienne Arieff says, "The fragility of not knowing if the clients will be around month-to-month is tough."

YOU HAVE TO BE THE BAD GUY (GIRL). A LOT. A mantra you had better learn early is "it's just business." Entrepreneurs need to mind the bottom line, and you will need to get tough with a vendor not delivering, an employee who makes repetitive mistakes, a landlord who hasn't fixed the heat, an insurance broker who wasn't looking into better options for you, a bookkeeper who didn't set up payroll correctly, and so on. It's your business now and that is a very personal (and potentially expensive) proposition, so, for the multitude of confrontations that will pop up over the course of the day, week, or month, keep your emotions in check and always put the company first.

YOU WILL BE SCARED. A LOT. When you own your own business, you quickly realize that you have no control over what happens in the world. Although, let's be honest here, job security for most, especially during recessions is an illusion. To be successful, you need to think long-term about your company and have a Zen approach to the short-term ups and downs. When the economy crashed in 2009, Chase Bank abruptly froze our credit line, even though we had a good record with them and needed the money to manage our cash flow. If we didn't have confidence that we would get another line of credit or develop a new piece of business to get us through the crisis, then that letter from the bank would have been disastrous.

EMPLOYEES ADD STRESS. The more people you hire, the more work you get done. True. But the more people you hire, the more weight is added to your shoulders. And the success of your business rests on you, not the employees, which is not a great feeling, especially when things are slow and you resent the people on your payroll who are taking home a paycheck when you're not.

YOU NOW RELY ON CUSTOMERS AND CLIENTS. This is a GOOD thing when you like your customers and clients but BAD when you don't. You cannot afford to tell the people who directly put money into your business to take a flying leap, even if you want to. Of course, if you or one of your employees is treated rudely, then you must confront the customer or client, but if you just don't like them, it is good business to suck it up.

YOU ARE RESPONSIBLE FOR KNOWING ABOUT TAXES. You must now be familiar with city, state, and federal tax laws that never before concerned you. Even if you hire an accountant and bookkeeper, you are ultimately responsible for knowing these laws. And for some people (us included) this is torture. Not knowing has gotten us in trouble, like the $1,000 bill we had to pay the state government for not knowing about the timing for paying payroll taxes. Rats!

YOU WILL THINK ABOUT MONEY. ALL THE TIME. Much of your time will be spent thinking about money. You will think about what is owed you, what you owe, what you will owe months from now, what you think you will make two years from now, what to pay yourself this month, having enough money to hire another employee, or starting a 401(k) account. When things are going great and your business bank account is flush, you will need to think about what to spend to make your business grow. When things are not going so well, you will think about how to spend less. You are now Chief Financial Officer for You.

The Unexpected Delights

When you are feeling as if there are no GOOD days, and the BAD ones are bringing you down, and you doubt your decision to make a go of things on your own, life often throws you a bone, like a new client or a huge order.

RESPECT FROM STRANGERS. When you tell people you meet at dinner parties or on plane trips that you own your own business, you will see "the look." Eyebrows raised just a little bit, a small smile, a nod that says, "Good for you." It is a nice response that you will receive from almost everyone you tell. And on a bad day it is a really nice boost.

HOW RIGHT YOUR NEW ROLE FITS. It will be amazing how easily you will fall into the role of entrepreneur. It will shock you how quickly you find your new rhythm. It will also surprise you how hard it will be for you to imagine working for someone else again. The feeling of independence you have each day is exhilarating.

THE SPEED OF YOUR WORKDAY. Your workday—although quickly heading for the double digits in hours—will seem half as long as it used to, because you now like what you do. You are happy and professionally satisfied.

THE RUSH YOU GET FROM THE LITTLE THINGS. You will experience a jolt of excitement each time you open the door to your own office or clothing store or studio or turn on your computer. You don't know what the day will bring, but you do know that it is all yours.

YOU WILL LOVE TO LEARN. You will learn about things you thought you didn't want to know in areas you were previously uninterested in. For some, this means learning to negotiate a good ad rate in the local paper; for others, it means learning the difference between a SEP account and an IRA. The only sure thing is that there is the opportunity and sometimes the necessity to know more about everything—from marketing to how to negotiate—when you run a business.

Are You the Girl?

We think it is important that while sitting at your desk fantasizing about the details of quitting your corporate job (come on, we've all done it), you ask yourself some important questions that will help determine if opening your own business is the right move for you. Chef Jody Adams, owner of the Rialto restaurant in Cambridge, Massachusetts, says, "It's crucial to evaluate yourself before launching a business, and make sure you get some help to do this. Enlist someone who doesn't know you personally, such as a business consultant, to ask you the tough questions and evaluate you objectively."

ARE YOU A PEOPLE PLEASER? You will need to please many people. Including customers or clients, investors, employees, vendors (when negotiating a little wiggle room for a due payment), or landlords. We had a former employer who hired people based on whether they had this trait.

ARE YOU ORGANIZED? You will most likely be starting out small, which means you will be your own secretary, marketing director, CEO, CFO, sales director, and public relations representative. You will be doing it all, so the more organized you are, the better able you will be to focus on the important details of running a business.

ARE YOU A PLANNER? The answer to this should be "Yes," because you will need to map out not just the business plan and launch of your business but a plan for next year, the year after that, and five years from now.

ARE YOU DIPLOMATIC? Let's hope so, because no matter what business you start, you need to be able to confront, defuse, negotiate, and praise when having conversations. For example, one of your employees has sheared the pom-poms off a client's champion standard poodle in your pet-grooming shop. How do you break the news to the client to appease them enough to prevent potential bad-mouthing? Or, for your new restaurant, your produce vendor (the only one in town) sends soggy mushrooms. How do you tell the vendor about what quality you are looking for without alienating him?

ARE YOU CONFIDENT? When trying something new, we all struggle with confidence (our palms were sweating during our first new business presentation); so if the answer to this question isn't "Yes" but "I'm working on it," that is fine. Confidence should be a goal for all of us, especially women going out on their own, because confidence inspires confidence, and you want your employees, customers, and investors to believe in you.

ARE YOU A RISK TAKER? This should be an easy "Yes" if you are serious about doing this. If not, then you might keep the starting-your-own-business fantasy as just that . . . a fantasy. There is no guarantee that your business will make it. Even if you chose the perfect concept, location, and team, a national chain may decide that you had it right and move in next door to compete for your business.

ARE YOU FLEXIBLE? You will need to be completely flexible with everything, from the flow of your money to the rate at which your business grows to the changes in the employment market. You will need to have plans in place for everything (see "Are you a planner?"), especially contingency plans for when business doesn't go as originally planned.

ARE YOU A HARD WORKER? Of course you are, otherwise you wouldn't even think about doing something like this. If you are not a hard worker—don't even think about starting your own business. Even if you work just three days a week, you will be working hard during those three days.

ARE YOU ABLE TO ASK FOR HELP? When you run a business, you need help. Sometimes you need financial help; sometimes you just need someone to mind the store while you run to the post office.

ARE YOU A GOOD LEADER? If your answer is "No," then add it to your list of things to work on. If you don't want to improve at this, then stay put or choose a business that does not require employees. To avoid excessive turnover and being faced with restaffing every few months, you want to be a boss that inspires as well as leads.

ARE YOU COMPETITIVE? Your answer should range from "Always" to "Like you wouldn't believe," because you can bet that your competitors are. Women have long been discouraged from owning this adjective, but we think it is time that changes. When we asked Carrie Levin, owner of Good Enough to Eat restaurant, if she had a daily mantra, she told us, "Competition, competition, competition."

CAN YOU LIVE ON A FLUCTUATING INCOME? We mean pay your bills, eat, take care of your family (and/or pets), and maintain your health insurance (very important) while starting this business. If the answer is "Maybe," that's not good enough. Go back to the planning stage and map out your money. If the answer is "No," then start saving before going out on your own. If the answer is "Yes," then move forward.

The Girl in the Mirror

Now you know a little bit more about the upsides and downsides of launching your own business, along with knowing more about yourself. We want you to stop reading. Sit down with this book and review your answers to the "Are You the Girl?" quiz. Ask your friends and family how they see you. Are you being honest with yourself, or are you answering yes because you are desperate to move forward? Now—before you have money invested and while you most likely still have a job working for someone else—is the time to imagine the worst. Could you handle a failed business? Can you provide for yourself and your dependents if business is slow? Do you have it in you to negotiate a reasonable rent with an unreasonable landlord? How do you really feel about putting in twelve hours a day for weeks on end? We don't expect that you know with certainty how you would respond to situations you haven't experienced yet, but take the time to at least think about the worst possible scenarios.

WHAT DO YOU WANT TO BE
WHEN YOU GROW UP?

To help pinpoint what business you want to start, you might want to try this visualization exercise. When reviewing your options for businesses, keep this checklist nearby. It will remind you to ask yourself the detailed questions in regard to each potential venture. Certain professions have restrictions or requirements that may or may not work for you. If you don't like public speaking, don't go into public relations, advertising, or marketing, because pitch meetings for new business requires you to do a lot of speaking. If you don't want to manage employees, don't even think about a retail store, restaurant, or any other business that can't be run by just you. When exploring a potential business opportunity, make sure that it fits into your lifestyle, needs, and personality.

Do you see yourself working

____in an office? ____in a gym?

____at a store? ____on a construction site?

____at home? ____in a restaurant?

____on the road?

Do you see yourself working

____alone? ____with an assistant?

____with a partner? ____supported by a staff?

____surrounded by a team?

Are you motivated by

____money? ____learning?

____freedom? ____challenges?

____power?

Your ideal work hours:

____All day ____7AM to 10PM

____9AM to 5PM ____10AM to 3PM

____8AM to 6PM ____other

Your ideal workweek:

____Saturday–Sunday   ____Tuesday–Thursday

____Monday–Friday   ____other

Your ideal number of workdays per week:

____1–2   ____5–6

____3–4   ____7

____4–5

How do you feel about public speaking?

____Refuse to do it   ____Thrive on it

____Dread it but will do it
    if necessary

How do you feel about managing employees?

____Delegate with ease   ____Thrive on mentoring

____Too critical   ____Would rather do
    everything yourself

Family Meeting

If you have a spouse, a partner, children, or other dependents, it is time to call a family meeting. Talk to them about your plan to start a business. Explain how your schedule is going to change and how it may impact them directly. To make this new venture work, you will need support from those around you. The early stages of planning your business is the best time to get your family involved. They will feel a part of the process and will celebrate your success. Carrie Levin told us that from day one her children knew what was going on with the business. She said, "Maybe I tell them too much, but at least they feel that at this point, years later, they are a part of both the good and bad days."

Now, Never, or Later

Though you have the enthusiasm for starting your own business, now might not be the right time. The reasons could range from *you simply don't know enough about the field to declare yourself an expert and start charging people for your services* to *you might need a little longer to pull together the funds*. Timing is everything in life and in business; so before you take the leap, see where you are in the process by reading through these statements.

Now
You will know the time is right to knock on your boss's door with a resignation speech ready when . . .

> You have the money.
>
> You have the time.
>
> You have the idea.
>
> You have the location.
>
> You have the partner on board (if you want or need one).
>
> You have the experience.
>
> You have the clients or customers.
>
> You have the confidence.
>
> You have done the market research.
>
> You have the enthusiasm.
>
> Your family is on board.
>
> You are ready to take off.

Later
Don't despair, you will be ready soon, but put the breaks on starting your business if . . .

You still have a lot to learn in your current job.

You still have a lot to learn about your chosen business.

You still have a lot to learn about opening a business.

You don't yet have an idea of the business you want to open, but you know you will.

You want more money in savings before you take the leap.

You want more time for market research.

You haven't found the perfect location.

You want more time to develop your client base.

You still have investment money to raise.

You are working on that confidence thing.

Never

You might think about staying where you are or looking for a job working for someone else if . . .

You like routine.

You don't like responsibility.

You want someone else to worry about bills, paychecks, taxes, accountants, lawyers, and bookkeepers.

You don't want to or can't work more than eight hours a day.

Your family isn't on board.

You can't survive on a fluctuating income.

Show Me the Money

When you start your own business, you may end up being the last one to be paid. Sad, but true. Because of your potential future lack of income, it is important to get a handle on your personal financial landscape before jumping into a business venture. We are not talking about funding your business. This is the money that you need to have in the bank to pay your expenses when you are faced with zero income.

Most financial experts recommend that when launching a new business, you should have a year of living expenses in the bank. This money is not used for business expenses; it is cash that will cover your personal needs before your business turns a profit. It may seem like an overwhelming amount to come up with, but that financial cushion can really help reduce the first-year pressures and give you one less thing to worry about.

To help you figure out how much you will need, fill out this monthly-expense chart. Be honest. If you eat out seven days a week, be realistic about the amount you spend. It will be a real wake-up call when you see how much you spend and how much you need to save before setting out on your own.

MONTHLY EXPENSES (WHAT DO I NEED?)	
Rent or Mortgage	_____
Car (payment, insurance, gas, tolls)	_____
Public Transportation	_____
Insurance (health, life, disability)	_____
Prescriptions and Personal Care Expenses	_____
Child Care	_____
Clothing	_____
Food (include all meals, snacks, beverages)	_____

Entertainment _____

Subscriptions (on-line, magazines, newspapers) _____

Credit Card Payments _____

Loan Payments _____

Utilities (electricity, gas, water) _____

Telephone (cell phone, BlackBerry, iPhone) _____

Household Care (repairs, cleaning services, supplies) _____

Cable, Satellite, and/or DSL _____

Gym _____

Vacation (average one year's expenses, and
divide it by 12) _____

Gifts (average what you would spend in a year
on birthdays, holidays, bridal and baby showers,
weddings, and divide it by 12) _____

Pet Care _____

Retirement Savings _____

TOTAL _____

---

the word

Galia Gichon, Owner
Down-to-Earth Finance

Galia Gichon, founder of Down-to-Earth Finance, offers what she calls "Unbiased Financial Education" services to a variety of clients. She is dedicated to advising women, although she works with men as well, and is thrilled with her decision to go out on her own: "As a child of two entrepreneurs, I always knew I wanted to launch my own business, but I am very conservative, and I wanted to do it only when I had everything in place. Before I quit my day job, my employer offered me a big promotion, which I didn't feel I could take, knowing that I would eventually be leaving to start my own business. So after many discussions with my family, making sure everyone was on board, I turned the promotion down and took the leap. It was the best thing I have ever done." With a third of her clients being self-employed, Galia knows what you need to do to get your personal finances in order before launching a new business.

How does someone planning to launch a business take stock of her personal financial situation?

The first thing is to know what your situation is. If you have debt, then find out how much. If you have investments, know what you are invested in. Track your spending for a month, meaning everything from the pack of gum you bought over the weekend to the movie ticket you bought last night. This may seem simple, but most people don't know how much they owe, spend, or are invested in. I call this a financial checkup. Now create a balance sheet based on what your financial life is today.

How much should she have in her savings?

You should have at least one year of income in the bank. This is your personal savings; keep it separate from your business finances.

How does she know how much she will need to live on?

The first step is to figure out how much you need to live on a monthly basis. You can base this number on the month of spending you tracked for your financial checkup. You will be revising this monthly budget, because once you launch your business, chances are pretty good that you will need to get that number down.

Do you have tips for getting that number down?

Since you will most likely be taking on debt when you launch your business, the first thing you should do is deal with your personal debt. Transfer outstanding balances to a low-interest-rate credit card. Keep track of your spending. You will be surprised by how much you spend. After tracking your spending for the financial checkup, review the categories of what you are spending on. Now is the time to prioritize your spending and make some changes. I don't believe that you need to deny yourself pleasure in order to save money. If you love eating dinner out, then bring your lunch to work. If taking a vacation is a priority, perhaps you could get rid of your cell phone. There are ways to save and ways to spend that will make the most sense for you. I also recommend that you do a checkup on your bills every six months. Maybe there are services you pay for but don't use. If you don't go to the gym at all during the summer, see if you can give your membership a hiatus until fall. You might realize that you are paying for a cable movie channel but don't watch it. There are ways to save, and keeping tabs on what you are spending daily, monthly, and yearly will help you find them.

Save, Save, Save

Are there ways you can cut back on personal expenses while you save for your own business? Absolutely. If you cook at home and go out to only one restaurant a month rather than order in every night (like we did), you can save literally thousands of dollars. And while you may start your day with a grande latte, make coffee at home. The ways of cutting back are endless; you just need to get your priorities in order. If you resent cutting back on your spending, this is something important to know about yourself, because the income fluctuation when you are running a business will be very frustrating.

Not Enough Money . . . Slow It Down

If you don't have the money in your savings to feel comfortable about launching a business right now but feel you are otherwise ready to do it, go ahead. But do it part-time. Many entrepreneurs start their businesses on the side or part-time. If you can afford to go to half-time at your job and your employer is willing to cut you back, then that will free up some of your time to focus on your budding business. If you can't afford to go to part-time at work, then take advantage of the evenings and weekends to do as much of your business planning as possible. Knowing you are spending at least part of the week focusing on your future will make going to work during the planning stages bearable . . . we hope.

Inspiring Statistics

From the Center for Women's Business Research (2008–9 studies) . . .

- 10.1 million firms are owned by women.

- Women-owned firms in the United States employed more than thirteen million people and generated $1.9 trillion in sales.

- One in five firms with revenue of $1 million or more is owned by a woman.

Wow.

TEN CHICK FLICKS TO INSPIRE YOU

It is sad to say that putting this list together was a challenge. Why aren't there more movies out there featuring women who own their own businesses? Just think of the potential for drama—love, loss, laughter—inherent in the situation. Must be just us because we could only come up with a handful. Some silly and some fun but all inspirational in their own way.

Mamma Mia!

Who doesn't love Meryl Streep? And this movie has her character, Donna, singing, dancing, and running a successful hotel on a small Greek island. Sure it's silly, but Donna is a hardworking single parent of her betrothed daughter, and we can be inspired by that. If not, there's always "Dancing Queen."
Inspiration Level: $$

Saving Grace

A pampered widow named Grace (Brenda Blethyn) discovers—after her husband's death—that he has mortgaged their life to the hilt and that she's on the brink of financial ruin. In the spirit of "pull yourself up from your bootstraps," with the help of her gardener she overcomes this hardship by using her greenhouse to grow major amounts of marijuana. OK, so it's illegal ingenuity. Still, we'll take that over buckling: Grace saves herself by starting her own business.
Inspiration Level: $$$ (was $$$$, but there are drugs so we had to take away a dollar sign)

Beauty Shop

Queen Latifah is strong, funny, and smart in this confection of a movie. Her character, Gina, opens the shop to give the women in the community a place to meet, talk, and laugh about life, work, and love. The supporting cast is great, but it's really the energy of the salon that's infectious.
Inspiration Level: $$$

The Holiday

This movie has almost nothing to do with running a business, but here's why we included it in the list. A good 50 percent of the movie takes place in Los Angeles, in Cameron Diaz's amazing house—you know, the one that she pays for by working her butt off as a movie-trailer editor? Love that.
Inspiration Level: $$

Mystic Pizza

One of our favorites from back in the day. Surrounded by a trio of young stars playing her employees—Julia Roberts, Annabeth Gish, Lili Taylor—Leona (Conchata Ferrel) is the owner of the local pizza parlor. Although each of the characters makes questionable decisions, at the end of the day it's the great advice and support they get from the women in their lives (mostly Leona) that straightens everyone out.

Inspiration Level: $$$$

The Women

Mary Haines (Meg Ryan) seems to have the perfect life until her husband dumps her for a much younger woman. After hitting rock bottom, Mary pulls herself together to be a better mother to her daughter and to rediscover her professional independence as a clothing designer. After the makeover of the century, Mary whips out a line of clothing, hosts a fashion show, and becomes an overnight sensation. Sure it isn't usually that easy . . . but it's nice to dream!

Inspiration Level: $$$

Baby Boom

J. C. (Diane Keaton) falls off the corporate ladder when she "inherits" a child from a relative who has passed away. Adapting to her unfamiliar role as parent, she opts out of her yuppie lifestyle and finds love, friendship, and financial success with a baby food business she launches out of her new (to her) but dilapidated farmhouse. It is funny, charming, and inspiring for those wanting a little boost.

Inspiration Level: $$$$

Sliding Doors

Helen (Gwyneth Paltrow) dives into launching her own public relations business in London. She applies for a loan, finds office space, and handles the launch of a hot new restaurant. Gwyneth makes it look easy and stylish at the same time.

Inspiration Level: $$$$

Chocolat

Guided by fate, Vianne (Juliette Binoche) arrives at a small French village with her daughter in tow and opens a chocolate shop. Although the conservative village folk resent her at first, Vianne and her mysterious chocolates are able to spark their passions and break repressive traditions. Watching Vianne's store come together is exciting. Be sure to watch this one with some chocolates nearby.

Inspiration Level: $$$

Places in the Heart

After her husband passes away, Edna (Sally Field) is left to run a Texas cotton farm that is quickly running into the ground during the Depression. Relying on her own smarts and some help from friends and employees, she turns everything around for her family. Watch Edna blossom as a businesswoman at a time when women weren't farmers.

Inspiration Level: $$$$

---

girl talk | **Jenny Maxwell, Partner and Cofounder**
The Cat's Pajamas

Longtime friends and roommates Lynn Deregowski and Jenny Maxwell wanted to start a business together. Having decided that they didn't enjoy working for other people, they knew only that they each had enough faith in themselves and in each other to make a business work. They just didn't know what kind of business.

Their road map to success was strategic, smart, and doable.

At the end of the day Lynn and Jenny met in their kitchen and each presented one business idea. "They ranged from opening a tutoring service to running a B and B, but nothing inspired both of us until Lynn came in one night with the idea to start a women's sleepwear company. Then we said, 'That's it!' "

Identifying the business was just the first step, because neither of them had experience in the garment industry. "The next step was for us to each find a job in the garment business. The level was unimportant; we just needed to learn everything we could about the business. And once we learned everything we could in one position, the agreement was that we would quit and find another job with another company that would teach us something else." During that time Lynn had three jobs and Jenny had two.

Was it frustrating to work for someone else, to answer phones and file, when they knew within a year that they would be running their own office? "Absolutely not. Even if we were answering phones, we learned something about customer service. We saw each job as a fantastic opportunity to learn everything about the business from the inside. We learned about how we didn't want to run a business, didn't want to treat employees or customers, and we learned a little bit about how to do it right. When you know you are going to start a business, every little thing is fascinating." They launched The Cat's Pajamas, a women's sleepwear company specializing in pajamas with vintage patterns.

What are the benefits of running your own business?
Neither of us likes being told what to do. We are motivated and enthusiastic about what we do; we don't need to have someone over our shoulder directing us. At this point we couldn't imagine going back to work for someone else. I am completely addicted to the flexibility in my workday. In fact, I haven't set an alarm in five years. I know when I work best and when I don't, and if that means working eleven AM to

eight PM, then that's my schedule for the day. We are both so driven by the business that there is no concern that either of us will slack off.

Tell us about your partnership.

In a well-balanced partnership like ours, each of you brings different skills to the table. I take care of the bookkeeping and insurance; Lynn takes care of the web site development and anything having to do with the computer. We are both comfortable with the company's rate of growth. We have respect for each other's opinions. If Lynn doesn't feel comfortable with an opportunity, we pass, no hard feelings. If I don't feel comfortable, we pass. We have complete trust that the decisions each of us makes on behalf of the company are the right ones to make. We share some of the not-so-glamorous jobs, like going to trade shows all over the country. And most important, we enjoy each other's company, and that is crucial, because we do everything together.

How do you overcome fears that may arise because of a slow period or a potential confrontation?

I have two methods for overcoming my fears. The first is talk to Lynn. We have such a great partnership that if I am down about something, she can pick me back up and reenergize me. And I try to do the same for her. My second method for overcoming my fears is to talk to other professionals. If I am terrified of negotiating a price with a vendor, then I run it by my contacts in the industry to get some professional advice. Getting validation from other professionals goes a long way to help make me feel better. Support is out there, and people love to give advice, because it often makes them feel better about what they have accomplished.

What are some of the negatives about running your own business?

When you run a small business, there are so many things that are not in your control, and it is important to develop a comfort level with this. You need to let a lot go and have faith in a lot of strangers. This is not always easy. It is also not easy to relax. When you work for someone else, you are not invested in the business as a whole. You can and do walk away every night and go on with your life. When you own your business, it is not so easy to walk away from it, even for a night. Also, everything business-related is now personal. This is challenging, especially for those women going into the garment business, because everything you are offering customers is something you have created. We will sit in our booth at some trade show and inevitably someone will come in and ask us why someone would ever wear such an ugly pattern. And we made it! That can be tough.

Do you have some advice for those women considering starting a business?

Know what you are getting into before you take the leap. So many people are excited by only one aspect of running a business, and they don't do the research necessary to find out about the bigger picture. Lynn and I lecture at local colleges for students who are interested in starting a business. We hear things like, "I want to open a restaurant because I really like to eat out and I know what makes a great meal." Making the meal is about two percent of what goes into running a restaurant. Staffing, marketing, finding produce vendors, stocking issues, all of this is what takes up the day of a restaurateur. So I strongly advise that you find out as much as you can about the entire business before you commit yourself to it.

Any last thoughts you would like to share?
There can be great days and there can be tough days, but if something goes wrong with our business, all I have to do is read the paper and I realize my life is a cakewalk. This will always give you a perspective on problems. And also, I really believe that everything always seems to work out in the end.

2

What Business Is Right for You?
And the Baby Steps to Make It Happen

Dog walking or dress design—what kind of business should you start? You've completed the personality test, passed the financial checkup, asked friends and family for advice, assessed your confidence level, planned, worried, and generally decided it's now or never. Now what? Quit your day job and hang out your shingle? Sometimes it's just that easy.

Betty McWillie, master career counselor and founder and president of Career Directions in Memphis, Tennessee, has been counseling clients about career changes for more than twenty years: "Clients come to me looking for a job change. After a few questions, it becomes apparent that they have already taken the steps necessary to start their own businesses. Many have been doing contract work on the side for years, and it just never occurred to them that they didn't need a corporate infrastructure to do the same job."

But for most people, it takes a little more planning and research to find and start the business that's right—one uniquely suited to your talents, interests, job experience, and that has a chance of being successful. This book isn't meant to encourage you to make the leap and fall on your face. We're priming you for success (see Chapter 4 for more about measures of success).

So what's the next step?

The entrepreneurial landscape can be sorted into businesses that require money to start up (capital investment) and those that don't. For now, let's assume you can always get the money, and instead let's spend time exploring your job history and interests, looking for the next move. This inventory is meant to focus your entrepreneurial efforts, because as Betty McWillie says, "There's a vast difference between a dream and a realistic business."

the word

**Betty McWillie,
Master Career Counselor and Founder**
Career Directions

Betty started her business in Memphis, Tennessee, after she went through a divorce. She had been a career counselor in universities and had always done résumé consultation on the side. After her divorce nothing seemed to be a risk anymore—least of all starting her own business. In fact, because of her divorce, she realized the only person she could count on was herself. She needed more income, and her side projects began to escalate, so she started her own practice. Currently, her career counseling practice is split fifty-fifty, women to men. Among her women clients, she has noticed a couple of common traits of successful women entrepreneurs, and she shares them with us.

All of the entrepreneurs I have worked with have a real strong creativity, enjoy independence, and are challenged by variety. They are generally very accomplished in their career field already. In a sense, they have taken ownership of their job before they left.

They have strategic minds and grasp the bigger picture, especially how the details are tied to the bottom line. I caution all my clients—it always boils down to finances. Do the math. If you can make it on your own, then why not try?

Look in Your Closet: Personal Interests, Experience, and Contacts

Are you successful in your current job?

The answer had better be yes. Even if you can't stand your boss, the industry, your commute, or your coworkers, you should be able to honestly say that you are good at what you do.

If you are happy in your current profession, investigate if there is freelance or contract work available that won't be a conflict of interest.

If it's available, take it—immediately. For Anita Katzen, a partner at Ellenbogen Rubenstein Eisdorfer and Co., LLP, when she was just starting out as an accountant, she would do tax returns for friends in her spare time. She began building her own client list that she was able to take with her when she opened her own shop.

Moonlighting gives you many of the core competencies needed by an entrepreneur. Not only does it provide access to clients and income for your new business, it also gives you a great look at the marketplace— valuable market research. Contract work will also add extra work hours to your current schedule and force you to organize your time. Finally, the economics of the industry will become apparent, which is important for planning the break to full-time freelance work. Most people are quite surprised at how high the hourly fee is for work you already do as a salaried employee.

Join professional organizations and start networking.

You will be surprised at how many unknown and highly active professional organizations exist. A two-minute Internet search provides a big list. Cut hair in Montana? Join the Montana State Cosmetologists Association. Own a dry cleaner in Delaware? Join the Pennsylvania and Delaware Cleaners Association. Design and create custom clothing? Join the Professional Association of Custom Clothiers.

Do some research on the organization. Choose one that will offer the most opportunity to meet people who will be future clients. Remember, you're not looking for a new employer; you are looking for a market for your services or product.

Use your current position to access information about the competition.

You are in the perfect position to assess the competition. Call in other contract employees and interview them. Ask what their rates are and what services they offer.

What if you realize you hate everything about your current job and industry?

You spend years in college planning for your career, work like crazy to get that first job, then realize it's nothing like what you thought it was and nothing like what you want. Okay, so think about other job experiences in your life.

Was there a part-time job where you thrived?

You worked your way through college with a customer-service gig. At the time, it was just a way to pay the bills. In retrospect, it was a job that you were good at and enjoyed. Is there an opportunity for a new business? Maybe, but more important, there was a set of skills you mastered and an environment where you excelled. Make a list of all the things you liked about the part-time job, and then brainstorm opportunities that use the same skills. For example, traits of a customer-service position include interacting with people, good communication skills, problem-solving abilities, and multitasking.

Do you have a hobby you love, and could there be a market for the product you create?

Knit, sew, paint, fix cars, take pictures, make videos, play video games, sail, ski, smoke fish? Seriously, anything you love can be turned into a business. Maybe not right away, but in baby steps.

A friend and client, Naomi Duguid (cookbook author, photographer, and world traveler) had a successful career in Toronto as a labor lawyer, which never quite satisfied her. A lifelong traveler, she spent all of her vacation time abroad, going places many people had never been. She always carried a camera and took a lot of pictures. While trekking in Nepal, she met another traveler and avid amateur photographer, Jeffrey Alford. They fell in love, joined forces, pooled their photograph collection, and started a stock photo agency, Asia Access. She quit the law, and from there, their collaboration evolved as they added their other passion to their professional life. In addition to taking photos on their travels, they were always collecting recipes from local people. A friend convinced them to write a cookbook proposal pairing their recipes and location photographs. They found an agent who sold the book concept to a publisher. *Flatbreads and Flavors: A Baker's Atlas* was named book of the year by two professional organizations when it was published in 1996.

Finally, consider your long-term goals.
Do you want to get married and have a family? Travel the world? Spend six months in the mountains and six months at the beach? All are doable, with preparation—but how do you prepare?

Baby Steps: How to Turn Your Idea into a Viable Business

You've come up with an idea for a successful business and need to get it off the ground. What are the first steps? It's time for DD—due diligence. First, do you have the experience you need to start (and run) this business? If not, then go out and get some. Take a part-time job in the industry—working weekends in a restaurant is the only way to see what it really takes to run one. In her book, *Wife of a Chef*, Courtney Febbroriello explains that her evolution into a restaurant owner in Simsbury, Connecticut, was really an accident. She had paid her way through a graduate degree in psychology with restaurant work. At one of her restaurant jobs, she met and fell in love with the chef. They married and decided to open their own place. Money was tight, and she ended up pitching in—raising the money, waitressing, hosting, hiring, firing, paying bills, handling the payroll. Eventually she realized this was the business she wanted. She also realized that her husband, while a great chef and personality, was a terrible businessman. People tell her all the time how great it must be to own a restaurant and be married to a chef. She smiles and nods and thinks that if they had to walk a mile in her shoes, they would certainly have a different take on the situation. Take her advice; walk the mile before making any decisions.

Then revisit the finances. Is it a business that requires a capital outlay? Do you have the money? If not, how are you going to get it? Check out Chapter 3 to investigate all of your financing options.

If the business doesn't require capital, what does it need? A service business needs clients. How and where are you going to find them? Time for market research. See "Market Research Know-how" later in this chapter (p. 41).

You will also need a place to work. We started in home offices to keep overhead low. Home offices have obvious advantages. In addition to cost-savings, you will be close to your work—a real luxury when you're working fourteen-hour days. But it's important when using a home office to take your work seriously.

TEN TIPS FOR WORKING AT HOME

1. Keep a schedule
Turn off the alarm, get up, take a shower, have breakfast, and get to work. If you're work requires you to interact with clients in an office, then try to keep to the same schedule as your clients do.

2. Get a good night's sleep
Just because no one will see those telltale bags under your eyes doesn't mean you shouldn't take your work seriously and be at your best.

3. Leave it at the office

You need a personal life. Set deadlines and office hours. When you are done, close the door, even if it's just to your office armoire, until the next morning.

4. Keep the television off

Minimize distractions. If you need background noise to keep you company, then go ahead and keep the TV on low, but if you find yourself drifting away, turn it off.

5. Get a babysitter

You can not do it all, even if that was your intent when you started your business. Arrange for child care at least a couple of hours a day. Or, if possible, do some of your work at night, after the kids have gone to bed.

6. Take a break

You need a break during the day, especially when you work at home alone. So, eat lunch away from your desk, go to the gym, read a trashy book, or take a walk. Do whatever it takes to relax and recharge yourself.

7. Be discreet

You may be working from home, but you don't need to remind people of it. Sure it's okay to get the laundry done during the workday; just don't let clients know that's what you're doing.

8. Dedicated lines and business e-mail

Establish separate phone lines for your business and personal lives. Don't let your child or significant other answer the business line. Where e-mail is concerned, select a professional name.

9. Get out

You need to get out of the house at least once a day. Try to make weekly appointments with clients or meet someone for lunch.

10. Don't surf

The Internet can be fun, informative, inspiring, and a big, fat time suck. Think of it like you would the television, as the place you go for a break. If you use it for research, then focus on the assignment and don't listen to that voice telling you that it will just take a second to scope out what your high school boyfriend has been up to.

What if a Home Office Isn't an Option?

You are a psychologist starting a private practice and need a place to see patients or a marketing consultant who needs to have client meetings—where do you begin looking for a space? Betty A. Kincaid, president and founder of Southwest Exchange Corporation in Nevada, has been a Realtor for twenty-two years. She has sold residential and commercial real estate, and her current business is 1031 tax deferred exchange, which is basically a processing and holding company for those who are deferring capital gains taxes by exchanging one investment for another. (Betty saw a niche in the marketplace and jumped all over it.) She explained the rental process to us.

Before you even hire a real estate agent, you have two big decisions to make: (1) How much space do I need? (2) Where should I be located? Check newspaper ads to get an idea of what's available before you call an agent. After you have a general idea of what you want, then start interviewing brokers.

For start-ups who need a smaller space, check with your local economic development office (city or county) for "incubator" space that may be available. Incubator space is usually smaller in square footage, and in some areas the rental rate may be partially subsidized by the city or county. Another option for start-ups is to sublease space from a larger company until you get some experience and a feel for how much space you may need and the location that suits you best.

Betty recommends that you always work with a member of the National Association of Realtors. You want to use a realtor who specializes in commercial leasing. You can contact your local Association of Realtors for a list of commercial agents. Check out the agent's credentials. Commercial agents who have taken additional educational classes and meet other criteria, such as production levels and years in the business, receive a designation known as CCIM (Certified Commercial Investment Member). For a list of the CCIM designated realtors in your area, go to their web site, *www.ccim.com*. You want as much experience as possible on your side.

A good commercial agent should recommend locations, help you evaluate your space needs, negotiate your contract, and work to complete any tenant improvements that you request. In most states, you can use an agent who works exclusively for you, the tenant, but whose commission still gets paid by the landlord. If they represent the landlord, too, they are required by law to disclose that information. You will only have to enter into a written agreement with an agent if you are selling property. As the buyer or leaser you have no formal relationship with the agent. You have the option to stop working with them if you're concerned they won't be a strong enough advocate for your position.

Once you've settled on a space and begin negotiating the lease, keep in mind that everything in the lease process is negotiable, depending on the market and the landlord. The most common areas of negotiation include rental rate, annual increases, and tenant improvement budget.

When we were in the early stages of planning YC Media, we saw an ad in the *New York Times* for affordable sublet space in downtown Manhattan. Minutes after we looked at the offices—really, the rooftop deck—we put a deposit down. While our enthusiasm is a good thing to take away from this, the process is not. We were so excited about what we were doing that we failed to investigate other options or even negotiate for a lower rent. We would not recommend this because we ended up paying more than everyone else on the floor and were armed with only a one-year lease. But fast-forward ten years and we had an opportunity to do it all again. After five years in our own loft space, we decided to return to our subletting roots. Luckily, we learned from our mistakes and successfully negotiated an arrangement that actually didn't sell us out. We caution you to ask your landlord or your broker the following questions before you sign anything.

WHAT ARE THE SECURITY ARRANGEMENTS IN THE OFFICE? Make sure your building and especially office are protected from unwanted strangers, vagrants, and solicitors. Make sure you change the locks on your office and ask about the cleaning service. Have they cleaned the offices recently? In our first space the landlord brought in a new service; not only was the man a little scary, but we all noticed after a month or two that a few things had gone missing.

WHO IS ANSWERING THE FRONT DOOR? In the absence of a security system where individual offices can buzz in guests, who will be answering the door for the messengers, mail carriers, solicitors, and guests of others on the floor? In our first sublet situation, we sat closest to the door and spent the day jumping up answering the buzzer. However, we learned from our mistake. When negotiating this next lease, we took the desks closest to the door contingent upon another company supplying a receptionist.

WHAT AMENITIES ARE INCLUDED WITH YOUR RENT? This can be a wide range of items, so when going over everything with the potential landlord, we suggest that you be as specific as possible. In our first sublet, we were entitled to a desk and a chair but had to purchase file cabinets. We had to bring in phone and Internet lines but could share the common fax machine. In our second sublet, we were entitled to a desk, chair, bookshelves, use of a kitchen, fax machine, and file cabinets. We could use our landlords' wireless Internet connection, and they provided a phone system. Other amenities usually include electricity, cleaning service, a conference room, and general supplies (toilet paper and paper towels).

WHAT DO YOU HAVE TO SUPPLY? Our start-up needs were minimal, but confirm what you are provided and then start the list. Your shopping list could include phone, phone services, computers and network connections, additional furniture, and business cards and other printed material.

WILL THERE BE ROOM TO EXPAND? When planning your business, try to think a couple of years ahead or at least the term of your lease. If you plan on hiring people, you will need to have somewhere to put them. We made this mistake with our sublet office once because we rented only two offices. When we quickly realized we needed an assistant, the only place available was a cube on the other side of the floor. It was inconvenient for all of us.

WHAT KIND OF LEASE WILL YOU BE GETTING, AND WHAT IS THE LEGALITY OF IT? In both cases, we had a binding letter of agreement with our floor landlord. We legally sublet our space, but some places are more "under the radar," so make sure you know what you are getting into. If you rent a space in an office and spend a bunch of time and money outfitting it, you want a reasonable assurance that your landlord's lease isn't up two months after you commit. Additionally, try to get at least a two-year lease. You don't want to be renegotiating after only twelve months in business and after investing money printing up letterhead and business cards that show your address.

DO YOU HAVE FLEXIBILITY DECORATING YOUR OFFICE? Our first office had an attractive design scheme; however, we chose to paint our offices in our corporate colors of bright pink and light blue. It was a little thing, but we loved coming into that office each morning. When we moved into a new office run by two design experts, we lost our brand but gained a super-stylish backdrop that will impress anyone who walks through the door.

IS THERE STORAGE SPACE AVAILABLE? As a publicity firm, YC Media needs lots of space to store client files, DVDs, new food products, and most of all, books. And books are big and heavy. We ended up drowning in our first sublet, so when it came to our second space we negotiated additional bookshelves and storage in the back room.

ARE THERE WRITTEN FLOOR POLICIES? Generally, people are considerate; however, over the years we've had issues with various cotenants. For example, there was the officemate who brought a dog into the office and proceeded to encourage the dog to relieve itself on a wee-wee pad in the conference room—just before one of our client meetings. We also had an officemate who liked to walk around in socks and an officemate who refused to answer the door even if most of the guests were his. Even if there isn't a formal write-up of floor policies, ask if your landlord would consider distributing one. You will save yourself several annoying and uncomfortable conversations.

A FINAL NOTE: NEGOTIATE, NEGOTIATE, NEGOTIATE. Don't accept the offer without a little research. What are others paying in the space? Will the rent come down with a longer lease? Are there other spaces in the area and what are they charging? Even if you are in love with the space, don't skip this step. You could save yourself a lot of money over a one-, two-, or three-year lease.

Ready-to-wear: Buying an Existing Business or Franchise

For the most part, buying an existing business is less risky than starting one up from scratch. There is a proven track record, employees in place, and an established customer base.

Pat Boyer and her partner and husband needed a change. They were fed up with their current careers; she was the tourism marketing director for the local Canadian consulate, and he was a packaged-goods executive. They had recently relocated to Ridgewood, New Jersey, and began searching for business opportunities. They checked out franchises and met with every real estate broker in their town. The final broker they saw clued them in on an opportunity that was privately being shopped around. The local bookseller, Bookends, was for sale to the right buyers.

The sellers (also a husband-and-wife team) wanted to make sure that the new owners would keep the bookstore and take care of it as they had.

First things first, you need a good broker and a good attorney. When you buy a business, it's a whole new world. It's not at all like buying a house. Your broker should be able to educate a novice and lead you knowingly through the process.

The "letter of intent" is the first and most difficult hurdle to cross. The main components of the deal are agreed to in this letter: when the closing will be, what price you are offering, and how the purchase will be financed. In the Boyers' case, they also had to make sure the seller had no plans to open another bookstore within a certain distance of the current store.

After the letter of intent with the five or six most important points is agreed to, it goes to the lawyers and the contract process begins. The seller's attorney prepares the first draft of the contract. Once the letter of intent is finalized, the contract process goes rather quickly. The Boyers made their offer to purchase in early September and closed on December 2. Every single detail is included in a contract, including how the seller's web site, database, mailing list, and key contacts are transferred.

Don't forget to consider all the third parties who may be involved with your business. If the seller doesn't own the building and has negotiated a long-term lease, then meet with the landlord and try to assume the seller's lease. All you want is a name change, but sometimes it's not a simple process. The Boyers held several meetings with the landlord to prove their creditworthiness and demonstrate their commitment to the community.

Town and municipality zoning regulations can be tricky. Once you take ownership, you have to make sure that all the zoning variances that were grandfathered for the seller are transferred to you. Unfortunately, you can't pursue the zoning board until you take ownership, so this is a bit of a gamble.

If you purchase a business that has a long history in the town, do your homework before you make any wide-sweeping changes. The Boyers spent a great deal of time getting to know the other merchants and members of the town, introducing themselves and presenting their new ideas for the store.

Give the current staff a chance. Generally, you won't be contractually obligated to keep the staff, but it's always a good idea to give them an opportunity to keep their jobs. Introduce yourself to them and reassure them that you want them to be part of the new team—only if that's true, of course. Be sensitive to their relationship with their former employer.

A Note About Franchising

A franchise is a complete business concept that a franchisee licenses for a fee and pays a subsequent royalty on. The upside is that for your fee, you license use of a trademark, ongoing support from the franchiser, and the right to use the franchiser's system of doing business and to sell its products or services.

The downside is you don't have free rein to run the business. You are required to follow the franchiser's rules and regulations and will be checked frequently to make certain that corporate standards are being maintained. A world of franchising concepts exists. Do your homework about a franchise. A good place to start is by checking *Entrepreneur's* annual Franchise 500. They rank the top five franchises in 116 different business categories. You can find information about everything from dry cleaners and flower stores to vinyl repair, chicken wing stores, juice bars, and pest control. If you are serious about franchising, attend a franchise-and-business-opportunity trade show. You can go to *www.franchiseworks.com* or or *www.franchise-update.com* to get a schedule of shows in your area. In addition to your interest in the business type and financial reputation of the franchiser, be sure to investigate the corporate culture. If you are a committed environmentalist, for example, you might want to make sure that the franchiser shares a similar commitment.

Market Research Know-how

Market research is a tool for collecting information you can use to develop your marketing plan and assess the viability of your business. Your market research should feel like a beginning course in journalism when the teacher explains that each story should answer the five *W*'s and the *H*.

WHO will buy my product or service?

WHAT do I need to charge to be both competitive and profitable?

WHEN my product or service hits the marketplace, what will the competition be like?

WHERE can my customers find my product or service?

WHY is my product or service marketable?

How am I positioning my product or service so that it will differentiate itself from the competition?

You can do it yourself or hire a firm that specializes in market research for your industry. On the web *www.marketresearch.com* sells market research reports organized by industry, company, and geography that can be downloaded for a fee. Before you start spending money though, see if you can answer the questions yourself.

Amy and Sarah Blessing, sisters and owners of apartment number 9, a men's clothing store in Chicago, decided to open their store because they identified a demand in the marketplace. While they worked at p.45, a chic women's store in Bucktown, customers continually asked for a men's version of the store. There wasn't one, so they seized the opportunity. From their retail experience, they were well equipped to answer most of the market research questions. For the ones they couldn't, they pounded the pavement and traveled to research what stores were out there for men, what men wanted from a store, and what was lacking in the Chicago men's retail market. Then they trusted their sense of style and incorporated all of the information they gathered to create a unique store experience for their potential customers.

WHO WILL BUY MY PRODUCT OR SERVICE? The Blessing sisters knew right away that there was a market for hip men's clothes in Chicago because men told them so. They realized, however, that they had to get to know the male clothing customer, because his shopping habits are very different from those of women customers. Women shop for fun; they watch for sales and come in if someone sends them a postcard. Men shop when they need something and rarely respond to sales, advertising, or direct mail.

WHAT DO I NEED TO CHARGE TO BE COMPETITIVE AND PROFITABLE? Amy and Sarah visited men's clothing stores and the men's sections in the better department stores in Chicago. They also visited as many men's stores in other cities as they could to get a sense of pricing in the market. Then they factored in the cost of the goods, their overhead, and the profit they would need to create from sales, to set their prices.

WHEN MY PRODUCT OR SERVICE HITS THE MARKETPLACE, WHAT WILL THE COMPETITION BE LIKE? Because they were in the industry, they had many sources and insights into the Chicago retail scene and knew no other similar store was in the pipeline. Being first to market was a big advantage for apartment number 9.

WHERE CAN MY CUSTOMERS FIND MY PRODUCT OR SERVICE? This question actually has many layers for a retailer. (1) Where should the store be? The Blessing sisters knew that they wanted to be on the same street (Damen in Bucktown) as their p. 45 friends, so they searched up and down the street investigating lease opportunities. (2) Will the store have a catalog or a web presence? For the Blessings, not in the initial development. (3) How should the goods in the store be merchandised and displayed? Sarah was an interior designer, and because the store's design was extremely important, that and the Blessings' experience and merchandising skills were to their advantage.

WHY IS MY PRODUCT OR SERVICE MARKETABLE? There was a demand in Chicago for a hip men's clothing store, evidenced by all the requests the Blessings received.

HOW AM I POSITIONING MY PRODUCT OR SERVICE SO THAT IT WILL DIFFERENTIATE ITSELF FROM THE COMPETITION? In a couple of ways mentioned above, the Blessings' merchandising skills are superior and they were first to the market, so they are way ahead of the pack.

| the word | **Amy and Sarah Blessing** |
| | apartment number 9 |

Amy and Sarah Blessing opened apartment number 9, a retail store in Chicago specializing in men's clothing. They loved the concept because it combined so many hats they loved to wear—meeting tons of people, designing the store (Sarah) and window displays, sales, and public relations. They talked about the idea for about four months and then started writing a business plan. In the end they enlisted help from the Women's Business Development Center, in Chicago. They then went to New York and placed their orders, signed a lease, and soon after opened the door. From idea to opening day took just over a year.

Amy Blessing offered her advice about opening a retail store:

Work in the retail business before you open a shop—even if it isn't for that long. Try to work at a small store if that is what you are going to open.

Realize that at least at first, it is very important for you to be in the store all the time in order to figure out who your customer is. So many people think they will just hire people to be on the sales floor—but I don't recommend it.

Be able to identify and explain why your store will be unique within the area in which you plan to open. We have talked to a number of people who have asked our advice while starting up their women's stores, and not one has been able to tell us how their store will differ from the other stores in the area. Know exactly why you are opening and whom you are trying to reach.

If at all possible, find someone to talk to who is in the same business and whom you respect. We still call down to p. 45 and ask them for advice when we run into something we have never dealt with before. I think a lot of people think that retailing is just really "fun." Someone even asked me a few days ago if I just surfed the Internet all day. People don't realize that we have work to do, all day, even if there are no customers in the store.

As for marketing, know exactly whom you are trying to reach, and do as much as you can to find out the best channels. Some stores in this area advertise locally, and I think they get some response. We haven't had any luck with advertising. I personally like putting press packets together and think editorial press is so rewarding and fun. We don't really have sales either, because men don't respond to discounts. Basically men shop when they want—regardless of what you are doing to try to get them in! Ultimately I base our marketing around what I personally respond to, and that is definitely editorial.

| girl talk | **Laurice Duffy, President and Founder**
LDK Cleaning Service |

Laurice Duffy faced a career crisis. She had just graduated from a local college with a psychology degree and entered a very competitive job market. She had worked all through college—in restaurants, gyms, retail stores—and was no stranger to long hours. After college, she began interviewing for work in her field. At the same time, her parents retired out of state and she was forced to move in with her sister. She eventually got a job for a health-care agency doing collections. The work was difficult, the pay terrible, and she was just miserable. Laurice had recently become engaged and needed to save for her wedding. She started cleaning her brother's house on Saturday mornings for extra money, and through word of mouth, began adding additional clients whom she cleaned for on nights and weekends. One day her sister, who ran a craft business from their home, encouraged her to do the math. It wasn't difficult to see that cleaning houses paid her twice as much as her health-care job. Now the mother of triplets and pregnant again, Laurice has a staff of seven employees and a thriving residential and commercial cleaning business. We spoke to her about running her business and raising her family.

What was the business like when you started?
At the same time I decided to abandon my health-care job and clean full-time, my brother had a baby and needed child care. I began by working for them three days a week and cleaning the other two, plus my original Saturday. Exclusively through word of mouth, more and more clients began calling. I was still doing everything myself. I took the babysitting down to two days and picked up another day of cleaning and then hired my first employee.

Cleaning all day sounds like a tough way to make a living; why did you do it?
It was pretty exhausting in the beginning, but I never minded the hard work because I was always focused on building my business enough so that I could hire people to clean for me. At the time I could do four houses a day in a twelve-hour day. As soon I as could bring someone on, we could do eight houses. It just kind of grew from there.

Did you create a business plan or do any formal planning for your growth?
Not officially in any business-school kind of a way, but I was always operating from one in my head. I was constantly figuring out the number of houses to clean versus the number of employees I could hire at a set hourly wage. I didn't spend money on marketing, because new clients kept calling me. I identified the major challenge immediately—hiring and retaining good employees—and I knew I wanted to develop a commercial business to supplement the residential clients, which

made sense because we could clean houses during the day and offices at night. I went through the phone book and started calling local small businesses. I also did a door-to-door sales pitch for the office buildings close to my home. Little by little, those clients started coming in too. I would clean houses in the morning, the offices at night, and do the invoicing and paperwork on the weekends. In the beginning I did everything by hand—payroll, invoicing, the books—but now it's all computerized. You could say that I even had a five-year plan for the business, because I wanted LDK to operate eventually without me cleaning at all. I planned to (and do) continue to do all the back-office operations and work with the customers while at home raising my family. I was lucky it worked out, because when I was pregnant, I was put on bed rest for four months and ran the business from my living room sofa and my hospital bed.

How do you balance running the business and spending time with the triplets (and we won't address being pregnant right now too)?

I wish I could say that I had a system. At this point, things are a little all over the place. We have an au pair and my husband gets home pretty early, so I have some flexibility. I mix work time with mommy time, because customers will call during the day or one of my employees will call with a question. I try to keep the back-office duties on a schedule. I do the payroll every other week, billing once a month, and handle all of my own taxes except the quarterlies. For the first seven years, I did it all by hand because that's what I knew how to do—now it's on the computer, and it's just getting to the point where it's faster.

What's the biggest challenge in your business?

No question, the biggest challenge remains hiring and keeping a good staff, since there are very few people who want to clean houses. I have two supervisors (one of whom was one of my first employees) and five cleaners. I focus a lot of my energy on keeping them happy (right now they are all women). I pay them a premium wage, offer Christmas bonuses, try to remain fair, and listen to their concerns. I focus on creating a positive work environment for them. I keep my refrigerator stocked with drinks and snacks that they are welcome to when they pick up the cars and their supplies. Communication is also very important. I have created a list of expectations for all employees of LDK, and when we get a new client, I go with them to the first cleaning and show them the expectations of the client. I also have them clean my house as part of their training so that I can work with them to get the quality (and speed) that I am looking for. You have to remember that servicing someone else's house is very different from cleaning your own.

What's the secret to your success?
Staying focused on my goal, discipline, and organization. When you are trying to start your own business, discipline is the key factor. When you don't have to get up at eight AM, it's really easy to procrastinate until ten, but whenever I felt that way, I would remember my goal. I can still remember in the very early days when I was meeting a new client. The woman was staying home with her children, and I turned to Irene (my first employee and current supervisor) and said, "That's going to be me. Staying home and raising my kids." Of course, I needed an income too. So I would force myself to get up early and work late. In general I am an organized person, but when you have seven people out cleaning thirty-five properties a week, six days a week, fifty-two weeks a year, things can get a little crazy very quickly. I know where everybody is at all hours of the day and check in regularly. It seems to be working so far.

3

The Scary Stuff
Legalities, Licenses, Permits,
Financials, and Funding

A lot of legal and business matters seem either boring or intim-idating. But they don't have to be. As a matter of fact, the more you know about the nuts and bolts of business, the more powerful you will feel. It's as if a secret world has opened up to you. Want to know about the advantages of a C corp over an LLC? Need to know how much liability insurance your business should carry? How to calculate and pay payroll taxes? To be honest, we didn't know either, but these things come with the proprietor territory.

This chapter is full of practical legal and financial advice about start-ing a new business. This is the stuff that makes you a contender, the serious, government-is-now-involved stuff, the stuff that separates the . . . well, you get the idea. So our advice is surround yourself with professionals who will put your business on the straight and narrow and make it easy for you to sleep at night knowing that your company rec-ords are in order. Here are checklists of questions to ask that lawyer, accountant, and bookkeeper you will soon be hiring. We will explain what these professionals do and what they don't do. We will save you a lot of money by explaining all the little things that took us hours of unbillable time learning the hard way.

Hiring an Attorney:
How Many Lawyers Does It Take?

Many people hire attorneys only when they have a problem; we don't recommend that. Hire an attorney to not only help you get your business off the ground but to help guide you through all the legal issues that you will face as an entrepreneur. Get someone on board as a member of your "small business team" as soon as possible. If you have a legal issue, it is better to have someone represent you who already knows you and your business well. You are not planning to be sued anytime soon, so why hire an attorney? To begin with, you could use an attorney to help you establish your company as a legal entity. Beyond that, depending on what kind of business you decide to launch, attorneys can help you draft contracts with vendors or employees, give you tax advice, write threatening letters to those people who owe you money, and go to court on your behalf. Deirdre O'Brien, of O'Brien & Associates, says, "You might not need one at all, or you might need one for issues like incorporation, partnership agreements, trademarks, employment agreements, and lease arrangements." Your attorney can be a resource for you, someone to call when you are faced with a decision that could have a legal consequence.

How Do You Find the
Right Attorney for You?

Just as with every other key player on your "small business team," get recommendations from everyone you know and then some. Deirdre O'Brien says, "Get a recommendation. Don't use the Yellow Pages!" Ask your friends, your family, your business contacts, your former employers, and your former colleagues. When you have a list of potential attorneys, set up interviews. Put some time into preparing for these interviews, because you are, in fact, meeting with a potential employee. Make sure that the attorney you hire is a specialist in what you need because each business will have different needs. The attorney who incorporates your business is not the one who you want registering your trademarks or representing you in a tax audit (may you never have need for a tax attorney!). With attorneys, one size does not fit all, and remember to call their references. Hiring the wrong attorney is a very expensive and frustrating proposition. We could write an entire book on that subject.

Don't let these attorneys intimidate you. Sure they are wearing suits, but remember you are the potential client. They need to sell themselves to you. If they act as if you are wasting their time, move on. You deserve a little r-e-s-p-e-c-t.

---

the word	**Deirdre O'Brien** O'Brien & Associates

Deirdre provided some tips for enjoying working with an attorney: You have to trust your attorney. If you do, don't second-guess her, let her do the work. If you keep second-guessing, it means you don't trust her (or you're a control freak!) and you'll alienate her, so get another lawyer—for everyone's sake.

Questions to Ask When Interviewing Attorneys

- What kinds of clients do you represent?

- Do you currently work with any small businesses?

- How long have you been practicing?

- What is your area of expertise?

- What do you know about my type of business?

- What is your fee structure?

- Are you available for consultation if I pay you an hourly rate?

- Do you have references?

- Will I be working with you directly or with a member of your staff?

A Note About Attorney Fees

Keep in mind that, as with all consultants, you want to get estimates in writing before you give the go-ahead. If you find an attorney that you feel comfortable with and her references check out, set up an appointment with her to go over your requirements. You may need her to help you incorporate or apply for licenses. Then ask for a cost-estimate in writing based on the list of needs you generated. She will most likely charge you per hour for this meeting, but it will be worth it. If your needs are extensive, then ask if you can go on a monthly *retainer* with her firm. That is a monthly fee for a set agreed-upon number of hours available to you. If your needs are mostly routine legal matters, such as reviewing a lease or setting up a corporation, ask if there is a junior member on her staff who can handle these items at a reduced fee.

Last, meet with your attorney on a regular basis to help you manage the time she spends on your business. Deirdre O'Brien says that some lawyers "like to build goodwill with potential clients by giving them advice without charging for it—say, over the phone or sometimes at least one consultation and maybe a few short follow-up calls. Then when it is a real issue, the lawyer would expect to be paid for her time and the terms of the payment would then vary with the lawyer's and the client's means."

Legal Structures: Partnership, C Corporation, S Corporation, Limited Liability Company, Limited Liability Partnership

The legal structure of your business directly impacts the question of your personal liability, the amount of taxes you pay, and the paperwork you file with the government, so think long and hard about the ramifications of each of the structural options. Your accountant and/or lawyer will and should weigh in on this decision and tell you what the differences are in terms of your personal liability, control, and tax burden.

No business has to be incorporated. A good enough reason to incorporate is limited liability—you won't lose your house if your business goes under. O'Brien suggests that "from a tax perspective, it may be a good idea to incorporate." Even if you have to pay an annual unincorporated business tax, if you are a small business with the intention of remaining small, then one of the unincorporated options may be the best route for you. But if you are planning to grow your business, to work with a bank on securing a loan, to look for outside investors, or are concerned about personal liability, then talk to your accountant and lawyer about legally incorporating.

Unincorporated Options

Sole Proprietorship

If you don't have employees and the business is just you, this is an ideal choice. If you use your name for the business and you don't need a business license (to find out if you do, ask your county clerk's office), then there are no formal documents you need to fill out for this structure. The profits from your company go on your personal tax return, and all of your business expenses that are deductible are written up on a form called Schedule C.

If you choose to go with this option, there are a few things to keep in mind. Since you will be filing a Schedule C at the end of the year, you need to keep track of every receipt and go through your expenses carefully with your accountant or bookkeeper. The amount and variety of items that are considered deductible may surprise you. For instance, a cookbook writer can write off restaurants that she eats in for research purposes. Keep in mind that since you are paid by your clients in gross amounts (taxes will not be withheld), you are required to pay estimated taxes quarterly. Since neither you nor your accountant know how much you are going to make your first year, these quarterly tax estimates could be either too low or too high. Therefore, try to set aside at least 30 percent of each check you receive, because at the end of the year you may be hit with a big tax bill as well as penalties for underpaying your estimated tax.

Partnership

Although easy to set up and low-cost, Deirdre O'Brien tells us that "Straight partnerships are out of fashion these days because of 'joint and several liability,' which means each person is liable for the acts of themselves and the others." With a partnership, you want to make sure you have every detail of the arrangement spelled out in an agreement written and approved by your lawyer. Leave nothing to chance, because with this structure you are liable for your partner's negligence and debts and vice versa. For instance, if your partner orders ten thousand dollars' worth of computers from Dell on behalf of your company, you are responsible for that debt. Additionally, since you will have a business account with both of your names on it, you each can take out money without the other person's knowledge, so it may be advisable to require two signatures on business checks.

Another option is the "limited partnership," which offers two levels of partnership—general and limited. The general partners would be responsible for running the business and are personally liable for debts incurred or agreements made on behalf of the business. The limited partners don't control the company, but they share in the profits and losses based on what they put into the business (money and/or time).

Incorporation Options

C Corporation

In the past, this was the most popular choice for many new business owners, but it has recently been replaced by the LLC as the corporate structure of choice. O'Brien tells us, "As with any corporation, the C corporation confers limited liability, meaning the corporation is sued, not the members, and individual assets are protected, in the absence of special circumstances, like fraud." O'Brien says this option is "relatively easy and inexpensive to form but may be subject to double taxation." This means that the company pays tax on the profits of the company and then the shareholders pay tax on the money they take home from that profit. There are ways of getting around the double-taxation issue (see "S Corporation"), and it's best to discuss the ramifications of this option with your lawyer.

S Corporation

This is the option that our original accountant recommended (of course we didn't listen and paid for it later when we had to pay to switch our company from a C corp to an S corp). Her exact words were, "Why wouldn't you form an S corp?" Her enthusiasm was due to the fact that with an S corporation you maintain protection from personal liability and you avoid the double-taxation issue that often arises with a C corp. The S corp operates like any corporation, with the establishment of officers, directors, and shareholders, and you do need to file a great deal of paperwork. Like a C corp, it is more expensive to form than the unincorporated options because you need to hire a lawyer or accountant to file the paperwork for you, but for small businesses it is an option. Some restrictions apply though, and you should review the details with the professional who files for you.

Limited Liability Company vs. Limited Liability Partnership

The differences between LLCs and LLPs can be confusing, so we took our own advice and consulted an expert. Nancy L. Adams, a certified public accountant and partner in Adams & Salter, LLP, explains:

> Two organizational types provide greater liability protection than you typically find in a general partnership or sole proprietorship: limited liability partnerships (LLPs) and limited liability companies (LLCs).
>
> A Limited Liability Partnership (LLP) is a partnership in which some or all partners have limited liability, similar to that of the shareholders of a corporation. Because an LLP is a partnership, by definition it has at least two members. Some states limit LLP formation to professional service practices that require licensing, such as accountants, lawyers, architects, and/or similar professionals. The LLP can limit the liability of a partner for errors, omissions, or negligence of the partner-

ship's employees of other agents. The liability limitations vary significantly by jurisdiction.

A limited liability company (LLC) is a legal entity that provides limited liability to its members. Liability may be limited to the amount a member has invested, depending on the jurisdiction. LLCs are considered "hybrid" entities, in that they have characteristics of both a corporation and a partnership (or sole proprietorship, if the LLC has only one member).

An LLC offers a great deal of flexibility, in that it allows its members to decide on how they will be taxed: a single member LLC (SMLLC) could elect to be taxed as a corporation or as a self-employed individual, and an LLC with multiple members could elect to be taxed as a corporation or a partnership.

Because the LLC offers greater flexibility in deciding how it will be taxed, an LLC may be a better choice than an LLP. A professional practice could also choose to form a professional limited liability company (PLLC), in lieu of choosing LLP as its entity choice.

It is best to consult a professional to discuss your circumstances; laws in your jurisdiction could have a significant impact on what is best for you.

Hiring an Accountant:
How Many Accountants Does It Take?

An accountant is a crucial member of your small business team, someone you can count on for more than tax preparation. At the start, an accountant can help you create a budget for the launch of your business. She can help you break down your start-up costs, which will include everything from paper clips to putting up a web site. Accountants often work with bookkeepers, who help you with the day-to-day finances involved in running your business. An accountant will also help you monitor the financial health of your business.

The key role of an accountant is to prepare your tax returns and monitor your tax payments. She can make sure your payroll taxes are being paid and aid in tax planning to avoid paying huge amounts at one time. But as Nancy Forman, of Language Liaison, Inc., reminds us, "When it comes to taxes, you have to take on the responsibility yourself." Even if you hire someone to help you through the tax morass, you must be familiar with the basic tax laws.

On the subject of interviewing accountants, Galia Gichon, from Down-to-Earth Finance, gives us this advice: "You want to make sure they work with businesses similar to your own. Make sure you feel comfortable when they are answering your questions. Get references and make sure you call them! Make sure you know what kind of bookkeeping system they use, because if it is compatible with yours, it makes the process of filing the business returns easier."

Questions to Ask When Interviewing Accountants

- Are you a certified public accountant (that is, are you licensed)?

- What services do you offer?

- What is your fee?

- How often do you recommend we meet?

- How large is the firm you work for?

- Are you going to be the one managing and working on my business?

- What kind of bookkeeping system do you use?

- Do you have a bookkeeper on staff?

- Are you available for quick calls, or would you prefer that I save questions for our meetings?

- What kinds of clients do you work with?

- Do you work with businesses that are the same size as mine?

- Based on the needs we just went over, could you give me an estimate for how many hours of your time I will need every month?

Record Keeping and Filing: Keep Those Receipts

It's easy to save every single receipt, paid check, bank statement, and vendor bill. Save it all, because someday you might need it. And you never know when that day is going to be. Nancy Forman says, "Record keeping is worth putting time into. I was a really bad record keeper, throwing out every invoice once I paid it, never filing anything, and not making copies of any of my checks. Eventually I learned the hard way that it doesn't work to do it that way. You need to establish a system from day one."

With the new computer you just bought for your business, you can use a computerized bookkeeping system by adding a software program such as Quicken or QuickBooks. Ask your accountant and/or bookkeeper what program they use. Once you have installed the program, input everything from bank statements to invoices and vendor bills. You may need guidance on how to do this. Use your accountant or your bookkeeper to get this set up right the first time. Then get in the habit of inputting everything. Dig that taxi receipt out of the bottom of your bag and input the amount into the local transportation column in your expense file.

Going green isn't easy when it comes to record keeping. Sure, we can view and pay our bills on-line, but we still need hard copies, especially if we're being reimbursed for an expense by a third party. Our bookkeeper, Martine Paul, recommends the following simple system: print out a copy of every bill, note the method of payment (on-line, check number, wire transfer, etc.), whether it is a billable or nonbillable expense, and to whom it should be charged back. Save all the backup for at least three years.

Create a filing system for all bank statements, paid checks, and bills. Even if you pay bills on-line, you will receive statements from vendors in the mail, so file those. Elaine Haber, founder of Jesco Consulting, Inc., says, "All vendors should have separate files so you can easily find paid invoices, contracts, and other paperswork." It is better to get the files ready to go now, even though they are swinging there empty, rather than later, when you have the paper to file but not the time to do it.

When we realized that we had hundreds of receipts from FedEx, American Express, Oxford Health Plans, and Verizon that were paid months ago but hadn't been filed or billed back to clients, it took us days to get back on track. How much easier it would have been if we had made a copy of each bill, filed the original, and sent the copy to the client with our bill.

So set up a filing system early, and do it right the first time. Elaine Haber reminds us to place "the most recent information in the front of the file, so if you are looking for something, it will most likely be right on top."

The Tax Man
(Taxes 101: Forms, Filing, and Headaches)

The bad news is that you will have to pay taxes frequently. The good news is the more you know about taxes, the better you can plan, and that means you spend less time, money, and energy on the process. Because the tax burden on the small business owner is significant and constantly changing, you will need an accountant early on in the process of starting your business. You also need an accountant who is able to explain it all to you in a way that doesn't make your head spin. We love our accountant, and she is great at translating tax-speak into real-people-speak, but that isn't to say that we don't almost pass out every time she tells us how much we are going to owe the city, state, and federal governments.

Unless you are a sole proprietor with no employees, you must register your business and apply for a federal tax ID number. This is an employer identification number (EIN). You already have a social security number that takes care of tracking your personal tax liability. The EIN tracks the tax accounts of small businesses. You will need to include this EIN number on all of your invoices and tax returns. Ask your accountant if she will register your company and apply for this number. To do it yourself, call 800-Tax-Form, and the IRS will give you a number (prepare to wait; we were on hold for quite a while).

You will need to choose your annual accounting period, or your tax

year. To do this, check with your accountant to see if the corporate structure you have chosen dictates your accounting period. If not, you can
choose either the calendar year (January 1–December 31), which is what
you must do if you are a sole proprietor, or a fiscal year, which can have
any start date other than December 31 and includes twelve consecutive
months. We recommend following the calendar year, because that is how
you manage your personal taxes. It is easier to do business-tax planning
and paying in conjunction with your personal-tax planning and paying.

We wish we could tell you otherwise, but payroll taxes are a night-
mare. You must withhold taxes and pay them for yourself and all of your
employees. You must withhold federal income tax, state income tax, and
sometimes city income tax, depending on where you live, along with
social security and Medicare (known as the Federal Insurance Contributions Act, FICA). As an employer, you must pay a matching contribution of your employees' FICA taxes. You will also need to file
Employer's Quarterly Federal Tax Returns, and you will have to pay federal unemployment taxes. Sound complicated? Luckily, there are people and services to help you. If you have more than two employees,
consider using a payroll tax service. These firms charge you a set price
per employee and will file all the paperwork on your company's behalf
and pay the taxes owed, directly from your business checking account.
Or, you can use a part-time bookkeeper to help you just with payroll
(and Quickbooks has added an inexpensive payroll module that is easy
to use). She will figure out the correct amounts, fill out the relevant
forms, and deliver the paperwork, coupons, and checks to the right people. If you are one of those people who thrive when confronted with
these tasks, then, by all means, enjoy this aspect of your business. We
encourage everyone, even those folks who think they have this covered,
to check in with an accountant on a quarterly basis to make sure the
payroll taxes are being paid correctly.

Who Says Girls Are Bad at Math?

When starting your business you will have very little money to spend on
consultants. Maybe you have just enough to hire the attorney who will

file the paperwork you need to get started. If you choose to take on the bookkeeping tasks yourself, set up everything right the first time. Get the accounting software program that is compatible with your accountant's; learn how the program works or ask someone to help you; and by all means, input the numbers correctly. Once you get into the swing of using the program, you will feel empowered by the ease with which you can print invoices, pay bills, and track spending. It is exciting to create your accounts-receivable full-color graph and to see exactly which client is thirty days late in paying.

How do you know when it is time to hire a bookkeeper? Elaine Haber says, "I recommend that women speak to someone as soon as they are thinking about starting a company, to find out what you need to do to get organized. A bookkeeper can get you on the right track in the early stages." Hopefully there will be a point in the growth of your business when it is more cost effective to delegate the bookkeeping tasks. This is when you hire out. Ask your accountant about what kind of bookkeeper she thinks you will need. Chances are she will have a person in mind whom she has worked with over the years, and if there is a rapport between your bookkeeper and your accountant, that makes your life much easier when the complications of tax season come upon you.

| the word | **Elaine Haber**
Jesco Consulting, Inc. |

The key to a positive relationship between a business owner and her bookkeeper is good communication. The business owner should work with someone who makes her feel comfortable enough to be able to ask questions. There shouldn't be the expectation that the business owner should know the details of bookkeeping. There are no stupid questions. On the flip side, the bookkeeper should be able to ask questions of the business owner. And if paperwork needs to be pulled or details need to be explained, the bookkeeper should be able to ask for that. Ideally, theirs should be a warm and friendly relationship.

One final note on bookkeepers: While there are benefits to doing it yourself and there are benefits to having someone else manage your books, either way, you must know what is going on. You have a responsibility to your business to keep track of your money, so if you do hire someone, make sure they work collaboratively and will explain anything and everything to you.

FIVE TIPS FOR ENJOYING THE SCARY STUFF

1. Keep your ego out of discussions with your consultants
Listen to your consultants and be willing to learn from them. Elaine Haber says, "All of the consultants you work with should want to work with you to teach you what you don't know."

2. Look at working with lawyers, accountants, and bookkeepers as an extension of your networking
Because they are in a service business, the consultants you hire, from lawyers to bookkeepers, talk to a lot of different people. If they like what you are doing, they can help spread the word about your business. Remember that word of mouth is a powerful force in building a customer base.

3. Hire consultants that you like to spend time with
Since spending lengthy amounts of time discussing tax laws isn't that interesting for many of us, make it as fun as possible by hiring consultants that you like. Better yet, hire consultants that make you laugh. We adore our attorney and look at meetings with him as a little bit of work and a lot of fun.

4. Forecast for fun
Managing the legal and financial details of your business helps you plan for the fun stuff, like renovations and hiring employees. Galia Gichon says that "it can also help you tremendously when creating a marketing budget."

5. Apply your new knowledge to your personal finances

As you learn how to plan financially for your business, apply what you learn to your personal finances. Hire your accountant to manage both your corporate and personal taxes. This way you have an opportunity to ask questions from a professional familiar with your entire financial landscape. You can also use the accounting program you have adopted for your business to track your personal expenses.

The Cash: Creating a Budget and Sticking to It

The only way to create a first-year budget for a new business is by doing research. A lot of research. Since you are dealing with the unknown, this is the time to get to know the nitty-gritty of the business you have decided to launch. Talk to real estate agents about rents, accountants about start-up fees and licenses that you will need to apply for, graphic designers about logo creation; get quotes from potential vendors. Ask members of professional and trade organizations about their first-year budgets. Your general operating numbers are out there, so now find them. Deirdre O'Brien shares this: "The obvious common-sense thing to do when creating a first-year budget is keep the costs down. I worked from home for the first year to avoid office rent, and I did everything myself to avoid salary costs."

To get you started on your first-year budget, here are the categories you need to include in a start-up budget, as well as a monthly budget. Since you need to include a budget in your business plan, keep the numbers as realistic as possible to demonstrate to potential investors that you know what you are doing. Finally, it is essential that you know not only how much money you will need to start your business but how you will spend the money you do get.

START-UP BUDGET

Workplace Renovations _____

Rent or Mortgage (down payments) _____

Utilities (setup fees) _____

Marketing (for launch of business) _____

Bank Charges (setup fees) _____

Consultant Fees

   (attorney, accountant, bookkeeper) _____

Business Licenses and Fees _____

Start-up Inventory _____

Start-up Supplies _____

Specialty Equipment

   (specific to your type of business) _____

Computer and Software Programs _____

Taxes (payroll, state, city, and/or federal) _____

Insurance (business and health) _____

Professional Organization(s)

  Dues and Subscriptions _____

MONTHLY BUDGET

Your Salary _____

Employee Expenses (salaries and payroll taxes) _____

Utilities _____

Marketing _____

Supplies _____

Inventory _____

Rent or Mortgage _____

Insurance (business and health) _____

Taxes (payroll, unemployment, state, city, and/or federal) _____

Delivery and/or Shipping _____

Bank Charges _____

Consultant Fees _____

Travel _____

Entertaining _____

Auto Expenses _____

Raising Capital

If you don't have the money to start a business, your family doesn't have the resources to help you, or your concept is very costly, then you need to look elsewhere for start-up capital. Your options are extensive, however the credit crisis of 2009 has made it extremely difficult to get a loan from a bank, find investors, or receive government loans.

We have outlined here a few suggestions, with the caveat that the viability of these options depends on the kind of business you decide to launch. To open a monogramming company in your home, you don't need a venture capital firm.

Once your business plan is complete and you know how much money is needed to launch your business, there are some financing decisions to make. Since all fund-raising options have consequences, talk to your accountant, financial adviser, and lawyer before applying for or accepting any capital from anybody. Even if Aunt Sally offers you a thousand dollars and all she wants in return is "a little piece of the business," discuss it with your consultants.

A note about raising capital (debt *versus* equity): There are two things you offer your potential investors in exchange for capital. The first is *debt*. If you go to a bank and take out a loan, the money (capital) you have borrowed is debt. Your financing is the debt (loan). The second is *equity*, or a part of your business in exchange for capital. If you go after venture capital or other investors, then the capital you borrow is paid back in part (or in whole) by equity in your company. Your financing is then equity.

Debt Financing

Credit Cards

Entrepreneurs often put start-up costs on their personal credit cards, which is all the debt many have available. We've all heard about filmmakers maxing out their credit card to make their first film, which went on to win an award at Sundance. But the truth is that most credit card entrepreneurs end up with a pile of debt rather than a statue. You are not at the point of making a profit, so why take on such high-interest debt? Why would you want to risk your personal credit so early in the game? However, if you are launching a business with a signed contract in hand from a client, then using your credit card on a short-term basis isn't the worst thing you could do. For instance, if you start a public relations business and have just invoiced a new client for their monthly retainer, then using a credit card to buy office supplies until that first check comes is a smart way to manage cash flow.

The Bank

When you take out a bank loan, you are not promising the bank a percentage of your business, so once they hand you the check, it is yours to do with what you will. For many entrepreneurs with a fantastic business plan but without the personal means to launch their business solo, this is the ideal scenario. But you will need stellar personal credit.

The first step is to complete your business plan. Carrie Herrington, owner of the retail shops Farmhouse and Farmhouse Flowers, tells us, "Your business plan is somewhat of a guarantee to the bank that your business is going to be successful, so make sure you have spent time on creating a thorough, well-researched one."

The next step is to identify a bank that offers loans to new small businesses. Elaine Haber recommends that an entrepreneur start with the bank where she does her personal banking. Haber says, "It is important to have a rapport with a bank representative. They can give you guidance and feedback on your business plan, and if you are dealing with someone you have worked with in the past, it will help make the process a little smoother."

Before your loan meeting, know your business plan inside and out, and be ready to discuss it at length. Carrie Herrington told us that her first meeting with the bank was "really scary." It is scary. You are approaching an institution to ask them to lend you money to help fund your dream. So arm yourself with knowledge. Know your business plan, know your field, know your competitors, and be ready to sell the bank representatives on your business.

Nancy Forman secured two loans from a bank for her business. Her advice is that if you are going to borrow money from a bank, "have a plan for how you are going to spend the money. I have always been the person who skips to the end of an article without reading it all the way through. In business, especially when you are spending someone else's money, you can't skip ahead."

Think of the bank as another member of your small business team. You may have to go back to them in the early years of your business for new loans, so it is in your best interest to have a good relationship with your banker. One of the main casualties of the financial crisis of 2009 was the near shutdown of lending to small businesses. One of our credit lines was frozen while our interest rate on another one was raised, so getting a bank loan to start a new venture will be more difficult than ever. Unless you have stellar credit and a great past personal history with the bank, you won't receive a loan. You must also keep in mind that loans now take more than ninety days to close. Making government loans available for small businesses is a priority of the Obama administration in the aftermath of the crisis, and it will continue to be into the future. No matter what the state of the economy is, though, save yourself some pain and investigate those options before you even go to a bank. Government loans involve more paperwork, but you have a better chance of securing one because of the incentive programs.

The Government

According to the federal Small Business Administration (*www.sba .gov/recovery*) home page:

> The American Recovery and Reinvestment Act of 2009 (Recovery Act) was signed into law by President Obama on February 17, 2009. It is an unprecedented effort to jump-start our economy, create or save millions of jobs, and put a down payment on addressing long-neglected challenges so our country can thrive in the twenty-first century.
>
> The Act is an extraordinary response to a crisis unlike any since the Great Depression, and includes measures to modernize our nation's infrastructure, enhance energy independence, expand educational opportunities, preserve and improve affordable health care, provide tax relief, and protect those in greatest need.

The Recovery Act was signed into law because banks stopped lending businesses and individuals money. The Recovery Act was put into place so that existing loan payments could be met (by reducing fees on loans and in many cases helping to refinance them), as well as by pressuring banks to start lending again. The SBA web site is a great resource and explains in detail how to get an SBA loan and identifies which lenders are still doing business.

The SBA offers a variety of loan guarantee programs and each is designed with a specific dollar amount threshold as well as stipulations as to the business type and use of the money loaned. The 7 (a) Loan Guaranty Program is one of the SBA's most popular lending programs. While the SBA doesn't lend money directly, it will guarantee loans offered by private-sector lenders through this program. It offers a preferred list of lenders to help you apply to those institutions that are supportive of small businesses. The banks that participate in this program will submit your loan application and business plan to the SBA for approval. If approved, the SBA will guarantee a portion of the loan.

The SBA also offers a Prequalification Pilot Loan Program, which will work with a small business owner to create a loan application package that includes, if approved, a letter stating the SBA's intent to guarantee the loan. The maximum amount for loans under the program is $250,000.

If you are looking for a loan of less than $150,000, there is the SBALowDoc Loan Program. Once you have met a lender's requirement for credit, the lender then may require an SBA guarantee. If this is the case, the SBALowDoc Loan Program is your best bet. It requires a one-page application and the thirty-six hours it takes for the SBA to respond to the request.

If you are looking for less than $35,000, then the SBA offers the Microloan Program. The SBA makes funds available to community-based nonprofit lenders, who in turn make the funds available to small business owners like you. For additional information on any of the SBA loan programs, see the SBA's web site, where they are all outlined in great detail.

Equity Financing

Whether equity financing is appropriate for your business depends on how you form your company. If you are a sole proprietor, for example, you will probably not be an attractive investment to venture capital firms or angel investors (see page 72), because you are personally liable for your business. Your accountant can review your business plan and identify the type of investor its structure will appeal to.

Venture Capital Firms
These firms supply capital on behalf of their clients, as an investment opportunity. They look to invest in a company in exchange for equity in the business. This means they want lots of control—the U.S. Chamber of Commerce states 30 to 50 percent is not unusual—and a high rate of return. This method of financing was huge in the dot-com boom, when millions of dollars were raised by entrepreneurs from venture capitalists who believed the entrepreneurs' ideas were big enough to go public quickly and make everyone rich. As we know now, many of them were wrong. So how do VC firms work? As with a bank, you present a complete business plan to a VC firm for consideration. Look for a firm

that shares your vision for the company. If you want to maintain day-to-day management and control of your business, find a firm that believes in you. If you want to launch a business that sells fashion T-shirts but have very little experience in manufacturing, look for a firm that has backed several successful clothing companies. Perhaps the VC firm will offer consultation services as part of the arrangement.

In this post-dot-com and post-credit-crisis world, it is unlikely that the VC route is the best way to go for a small business owner. We recommend that you look to other sources of financing first. If you do go this route, then we suggest that you either limit the details about your idea in your presentation or have those you're meeting with sign a confidentiality agreement before you hand over your business plan—you don't want anyone stealing your million-dollar invention. We also highly recommend working with Springboard Enterprise (*www.springboardenterprises.org*), a not-for-profit organization that produces programs that support women entrepreneurs as they go after equity funding. Springboard includes fantastic information on its web site ranging from "Equity Capital Market Fundamentals" to "Creating Your Pitch."

| the word | **Monica Lee, Manager**
Springboard Enterprise and Center for Women and Enterprise in New England |

Springboard is the largest venture capital forum that specifically focuses on women. The Center for Women and Enterprise is a nonprofit organization supported by corporate, individual, and government funding that helps women to start up their businesses. Monica gave us the skinny on the big bucks.

Before you begin to consider venture capital as an option, you should evaluate if yours is a kind of company or industry that is even attractive to that market. To go after venture capital funding, women need to be in a high-technology industry, for example, computer software, biotechnology, life sciences (a broad term for *medical areas*), or electronics. They must also demonstrate a sustainable competitive advantage, either a patent or proprietary technology or some other barrier to entry—and something that can't be taken away from you, say a first-mover advantage, meaning you've already captured 60 percent of the market. The majority of the time the competitive advantage is a patented technology. You must also have a large market size, typically greater than $1 billion (we kid you not). Nowadays venture capitalists tend to be more conservative than they were before. To get this type of funding, you must prove that you are close to getting revenues or have revenues already and have secured some distribution channels. In their words, you must have achieved some traction in the industry. At minimum, one or two of these criteria must be in place. If you are a retailer looking for small sums of money, it's not worth going through this process. Seek other funding, such as bank loans or money from friends and family.

If you are going to go after venture capital, be prepared to devote one-third to one-half of your time to going after money. It's an incredibly time-intensive and exhausting process. Know what you have to give up in exchange. Ultimately, if you do secure this type of funding, you have to give over a portion of your company. The venture capitalist could serve on the board, have say-so on strategy, and could ultimately attain the majority shareholder position. You may be giving away anywhere from a couple of percentage points to a 50 percent position.

One of the keys to getting VC money is access and connections. Historically VC money has gone to men. Even if you look just at technology companies, you find the money has gone to men. It's really all about connections and who you know. Men tend to have many more connections, through business school or industry, and can get their foot in the door easier.

Angels from Heaven

An *angel* is someone looking for a new business investment. They can include people you know—vendors, professional associates, or employees—or strangers that you have been put in touch with through organizations like Active Capital, formerly known as the SBA's Angel Capital Electronic Network (ACE-Net), or investment bankers that represent small investors. You can even connect with these angel investors through your own outreach, including solicitation letters or networking with wealthy individuals who are on the lookout for opportunities with high rates of return.

Angel investors, like all lenders, look for great ideas, strong management, a complete business plan, and a potential high return on investment. If you find an angel investor, make sure that your lawyer reviews any agreement before you sign it.

A final word about raising cash: know your business plan, market potential, and yourself before you put yourself in front of any potential lender.

**TEN BUSINESS TERMS TO HAVE ON
THE TIP OF YOUR TONGUE**

Knowledge is power. Here are ten terms to add to your new business girl vocabulary.

1. **Profit:** This is the money your company makes after you have paid all of your overhead costs. Let's say that you have a graphic design business. You are hired for only one job this month. After you have paid yourself, the rent, the electricity bill, the staff, the insurance bill, for office supplies and shipping, any money left over is the profit.

2. **Marketing Plan:** This is the plan that you have created for how you are going to market your business to your key customers. It includes a budget for advertising, events, public relations, an on-line presence, and any other promotions you might consider.

3. Branding: This is the image that you have created for yourself and your business. This image should *say* something about your business to your potential customers. Ralph Lauren, and by extension his company, has branded himself as a designer who shares the good life with his customers through his clothing and products. To brand your company, first know what you want your company to represent to people and extend that through your marketing outreach, logo design, and products or services.

4. Markup: This is the gross profit above the cost of the product. If you buy a pair of fifty-dollar earrings from a wholesaler to sell at your jewelry store and sell them for one hundred dollars, your markup is 100 percent.

5. Target Demographics: These are your key customers, who will buy your product, come into your store, or hire you as a consultant. The *demographic* refers to where your customers can be found in society at large. If you sell gourmet pet food, your target demographic would be high-income pet owners.

6. Pretax Income: This is your income before taxes have been paid or might have to be paid. This is important because it may seem as though you are making a lot of money, but don't count on it until you see your net income number.

7. Net Income: What you have earned after all of your expenses and taxes have been paid.

8. Networking: As a new business owner, you are starting from scratch and you want and need to meet people in your target market face-to-face—so find out what organizations they belong to, join, and introduce yourself. Always carry your business cards with you.

9. Product/Service Differentiation: The factors that differentiate your product or service from your competitors'. You need to

> know this when formulating your business concept and plan and use this information during new business meetings.
>
> 10. **Competitive Pricing:** The amount you can charge for your products or services that is in line with your competitors' prices. If you charge more than your competitors, be very clear in your branding, advertising, and networking about why you and your business are worth it.

Insurance Primer: Get Yourself Covered!

When launching your business, line up a basic insurance package that includes workers' compensation, general liability, and property/casualty coverage. Look into auto insurance if you have a delivery truck or you use your car for business, as well as life insurance and disability insurance. Fidelity Investments Insurance (*www.fidelity.com*) and American Council of Life Insurers (*www.acli.com*) are two good resources for this type of information. This coverage is all in addition to your health insurance, which is an absolute must.

Health Insurance

Health insurance is expensive, so before quitting your full-time job to launch a business, check in with your company's human resource department about COBRA (Consolidated Omnibus Budget Reconciliation Act). COBRA is a law that gives certain former employees, dependent children, retirees, spouses, and domestic partners continuation of health insurance at group rates for a limited amount of time. Go to *www.cobrahealth.com* to review specific limitations and restrictions. Once your COBRA extension is up, you can sign up as a business owner with the current plan or speak to an insurance representative about other options that may suit your needs a little bit better. If you are married and your husband has health insurance with his company, now is the time to add yourself to his plan. If you are not married but do have a domestic partner, depending on the health plan of your partner and/or state regulations, you may be covered. We guarantee it will be less costly to be added to an existing plan.

General Liability

Most businesses should have general liability coverage because it protects you from anyone who has an accident at your place of business, as well as covering accidents that resulted from your products. This means you would be covered if you owned a sandwich shop and a customer tripped on a box of potato chips left on the floor and broke her wrist. You would also be covered if you made and sold lamps and a customer returned one because the shade got too hot and burned her hand. As with workers' compensation, the level of coverage is determined by the size and type of your business. You might opt for increasing your coverage based on the nature of your business. For example, if you are a graphic designer and you submitted a document that hadn't been spell-checked to the printer for a huge print job, you would be covered for the reprint if you had added "errors and omissions liability" to your insurance coverage.

Property/Casualty

The coverage of this type of insurance is outlined by the perils (fire, flood, theft . . .) that are listed in the agreement. Read the coverage carefully, and make sure all the perils that may impact your ability to do business are included. For instance, loss by fire is in all policies, but loss by flood is not. If you have opened a business near a river, ocean, lake, or any other body of water, you should look into adding this peril. If you own a business with a lot of equipment, such as a textile company, consider replacement-cost insurance, which would cover the cost of replacing your equipment.

Auto Insurance

This coverage is required by most states if you or your employees use cars to do business.

Life Insurance

Most financial institutions, venture capitalists, and angel investors will require that you, the owner of the small business, get life insurance in an amount that would cover the cost of the debt borrowed. In addition to paying off the loan though, this insurance should provide for your family, and can be extremely expensive.

Disability Insurance

This is especially important for freelancers who are sole proprietors. Should something happen to make it impossible for you to work, it is likely you will make zero income. We just heard about a freelance publicist who is having a difficult pregnancy. Her doctor has put her on bed rest for the duration of her pregnancy (five months, can you imagine?!). Luckily she has disability insurance, and she will be receiving a large portion of her income from the insurance agency. Disability insurance is sometimes called "income insurance" for a reason.

Workers' Compensation

Many states require businesses with more than one employee to carry workers' compensation insurance. Each state varies on what type of coverage is required and where it can be purchased. We buy our workers' comp policy from the New York State Insurance Fund directly. Investigate your options through your state web site or check out an aggregator such as *www.workerscompensationshop*.com as a place to start. Make sure you ask your attorney what laws apply to you. Because we started as a business with two partners and no employees, we didn't have to provide coverage by law, so we never knew to ask the question about what we were legally required to provide once we had employees. The state of New York was kind enough to send us a letter and a fine to remind us to comply with the law.

TIPS FOR WORKING WITH AN INSURANCE REPRESENTATIVE

Get a referral for a good representative
As with all professional consultants, you want to work with someone you trust and like and who comes highly recommended.

Outline your needs and bring the list to the meeting
Write down everything that you can think of that could happen to your business. Flood, fire, theft, gas leak, your death, your partner's death, fraud, hurricane, tidal wave, sexual harassment suit—nothing is too big or too small for this list. Your representative will take you through the options for coverage.

Ask for quotes from a few insurance agents so that you can compare pricing
Think of it as you would any other purchase, and find the right deal for you.

Home-Business Insurance

Even if you have homeowners insurance, get additional insurance for a home-based business. Why? Because the perils that may effect a home business will probably not be covered by homeowners insurance. If you work in the studio above the garage, it may not be covered in the case of a fire. If a client or customer comes to your home office and has an accident, you may not be covered if a lawsuit arises. If your basement is flooded and the water destroys your computer, fax, phone, copier, and printer, you might be covered for only a portion of the replacement cost of the equipment. Speak to your insurance representative about optional riders you can put on your homeowners or home-business insurance, in addition to the disability we recommend that you get. If there is an employee helping to pack up and ship your homemade candies out of your living room, make sure you have workers' compensation coverage. Last, if you drive clients around—for example, you open a real estate office and are showing properties to potential buyers—you will need to add business coverage to your car insurance.

A final note about insurance: Update it every year. If your business grows, your insurance needs may change. Buy only what you need; know the details of your plans; don't duplicate coverage; and make sure you are properly insured.

Licenses and Permits

For many businesses there are licenses and/or permits that need to be filed with the city, state, and federal governments.

Business License

This is a license that is required by many cities and towns for a fee (what is free these days, anyway?). The business license department will check to make sure your location is zoned for the type of business you are running. This is particularly important if you are running a business out of your home, because it may be illegal to operate a business there.

Health Permit

This is a requirement for a variety of businesses ranging from nail salons to day-care centers. It is essential if you are serving or selling food to anyone. This includes restaurants, caterers, takeout places, basically any and all businesses that hand over food. Check with your local health department on the details of this permit—including cost, application process, requirements, and inspection policies.

Fire Department Permit

If your business is open to the public, you will need to apply for this permit. Again, there is a fee involved and you will be inspected, so be clear on the rules and regulations.

State Licenses

There are certain kinds of businesses that need a state and/or city license (for example, manicurist and contractor), and some require testing in order to obtain one (for example, real estate agent). To get the complete list of who needs to get a license through the state and/or city, go directly to your state and/or city government web sites.

County Permits

If you are operating a business outside of a town or city jurisdiction, you may need to file a permit application with the county.

Sign Permit

Depending on where you open your business, you might not be able to put up the sign you want. Some locations have restrictions on size, location, and even type of sign. Keep in mind that your landlord may also have restrictions about putting up your sign.

Liquor Licenses

Depending on the state you open a business in, these licenses are usually split into a wine and beer license and a hard liquor license. And in some places it is not that easy to obtain one. Think about all of the restaurants you have been to that have a B.Y.O.B. policy. It's not that they are being kind; they just don't have a license to sell liquor. Before deciding on a business and a location, check with your local beverage control agency about rules and regulations regarding booze in your state.

Julie Castiglia
Castiglia Literary Agency

Julie Castiglia established the Castiglia Literary Agency. Prior to becoming an agent, Julie freelanced as an editor and writer for eleven years. As an agent, she has sold nonfiction and fiction titles to major publishers.

How did you become an agent?
I was originally a writer with three published books and a free-lance editor for a few years, so I knew the publishing business well. After I was divorced I needed to work, and this was the one industry I knew something about, so I answered an ad in the paper for an assistant to a literary agent. I was told that the job was taken, but they asked me some questions and said to come in and talk. I was given a manuscript to read, which I read overnight and told them I could sell it. That was the first manuscript I sold. I started working there a couple of hours a day in the beginning, worked my way up, staying until nine at night sometimes. It was a great way to learn more about the business, and my boss was a great mentor, completely unselfish. I made some solid business connections that I still have today.

How did you fund the launch of your business?
Since there wasn't anyone at the agency who could take care of my clients, they allowed me to take them with me when I left. Having a base of clients to work with allowed me to start placing books with publishers immediately. The first year was difficult, but after that things started to happen.

Did you have children when you launched your business?
Yes, I did have kids at home in the beginning. Running a literary agency is a great job for a woman with a family, because many

boutique agencies can be run out of a home office. Or if you do have an outside office—and I've had both—you can have a laptop and a cell phone and actually be very independent as far as picking kids up from school and switching over to a home office for a few hours when the children are at home. And of course reading can be accomplished very easily at home.

How do you staff your business?
I always use freelancers and part-timers. It works better for me because I don't need someone all the time. Sometimes I'm overloaded, and other times—especially in August and December—nothing much is happening in the business.

Do you have a mantra you say to yourself in times of business stress?
I try to look back to see what happened in the past when I was stressed over something similar. I keep notes and review them, so I can see right away that something that seemed so overwhelming at the time wasn't that awful after all and that all bad scenarios do pass. In other words I depend on past experiences when handling stressful situations. But I don't ever stay stressed for very long. In this business there seem to be stressful moments almost every day. Laughter helps.

Do you have any tips for dealing with confrontations?
You learn to be tough in tough situations, when dealing with editors, clients, and producers. You can't be a wimp, because you would lose respect. When confronted with a situation, I quickly try to analyze the reasons behind it and don't personalize it in any way. I take a deep breath and put on my most soothing and professional voice, even if inside I feel as if I want to scream and shout. Okay, I did yell back once or twice but not in recent years.

Was it hard for you to accept your success?
Success was a gradual buildup, so although I am successful, I've had to hang in there to make it happen. I make a good living, and I've built up an agency with some great clients and strong relationships with editors. I'm happy doing what I do.

4

Your Business Plan
*Why You Should Spend Your
Precious Time Writing One*

The dreaded, overwhelming business plan . . . where do you begin? Is it even worth undertaking? Every successful woman running her own business, from Oprah to your yoga instructor, has sat down at one time or another (or daily, in our case) and thought about the direction of her business. And that's really all there is to it.

Can you take on another client? Can you afford to buy out the competition? What increase in sales do you want to see in twelve months, in twenty-four, and in forty-eight? Writing a business plan takes time. Lots and lots of time. Before you begin, evaluate your motives for writing the plan. Are you looking to plan for the future? Are you seeking outside investment? If you are simply trying to get your goals on paper and make revenue projections, then do just that without working up a formal plan.

What Is a Business Plan?

According to the Women's Business Center, a business plan "is a blueprint of your company, presented in standard business format, that is logical and well documented." A business plan is used by entrepreneurs going after funding (as we outlined in Chapter 3) and by entrepreneurs who are self-financing. If you are one of the few technology or biotech entrepreneurs left out there going after the big investment dollars or even a small retail shop owner going after a bank loan, a perfect, polished, and professional business plan is a must. If you are planning to launch a service business and are not looking for outside funding, then you write a business plan to bring focus to your goal setting and budget forecasting.

It is essential that every entrepreneur create a business plan, no matter how small or large her dream. The Women's Business Center points out that "the success of your business depends largely upon the decisions you make. A business plan allocates resources and measures the results of your actions, helping you set realistic goals and make decisions." Spend the time creating a business plan that you can rely on as your road map for the next few years.

What Is Included in a Business Plan?

There are plenty of resources for women who need help writing business plans. You can go to *www.bplans.com* and download sample plans for a fee. Search your local small business office; find them at *www.sba.gov/smallbusinessplanner*. Or visit the Online Women's Business Center at *www.onlinewbc.gov*. Check out the National Women's Business Council at *www.nwbc.gov*. The easiest way to get a shell of a plan and all the necessary accompanying spreadsheets is to download a free one from *www.sba.gov/smallbusinessplanner* or *www.score.org/template_gallery.html*.

The Important Elements of a Business Plan

The key to writing an effective business plan is to do research, research, and more research. Writing a business plan will help you focus your thoughts about the details of the business, so skipping over items in the business plan because they are just too tedious will not help you in the long run—although it's okay to skip them for a while and return later. Keep in mind that your business plan is a sales tool that will be used to go after outside investors, as well as your blueprint to build a company that sells products or services to customers. To be an effective sales tool, the information has to be well researched and concisely formatted.

According to the Women's Business Center, a basic business plan should include:

Executive Summary

Market Analysis

Company Description

Organization and Management

Marketing and Sales Strategies

Service or Product Line

Funding Request

Financials

Executive Summary

This is the most important section of your business plan. In fewer than four pages you provide a compelling overview of your business plan and describe your company, why it is relevant, and where you see it going in the future. Because the executive summary needs to be so concise and detailed, write this section *last,* once you have compiled and reviewed all of your research.

At this point you won't have a whole lot of details to plug in (such as location, employees, plans for growth), so focus on your background and professional experience. Include a statement about the need your business will fill, and illustrate why you are the best person for the job. You're selling you, your business idea, and your expertise too.

What follows are descriptions of what should be the components of an executive summary for new business owners.

Mission Statement

A mission statement outlines your business philosophy and your business's services and reason for being, in a few sentences or paragraphs. It is the essence of your business. Mission statements are tricky to nail in one sentence. Don't labor over the words. Start by making a list of values for the company; just jot them down as they come to you. When you've got a pretty big list, narrow them down, prioritize them, and then develop the mission from your core values. Having a mission statement to refer to can help you make the kinds of decisions you will soon face— from hiring (does the potential candidate fit the business philosophy?) to marketing (does this magazine we are considering advertising in represent what we are all about?). We haven't completely nailed our mission statement, however we've got our values down. We value excellence and inspiration. We aim to work with clients whose brands inspire us and teach us. We want them to be the best in their field and are constantly working to improve their brand.

Start Date

This is fairly self-explanatory. Even if you are going after funding, you will have needed to file the paperwork necessary to register your business as a legal entity. So write in the date.

Founders and Their Roles

Keep it brief. Just list names and titles. You'll get into specifics later in the plan.

Number of Employees

List the total number of employees; you will get to their roles later in the plan. If you are planning to hire employees in the future but need funding to make it happen, include that number in here anyway to provide a snapshot of your business potential.

Location

If you don't have a location and will be looking for one soon, add it when you get it. If you've found the location, add a paragraph, "Description of

Facilities," and list the rooms, windows, equipment, and number of bathrooms. If you are opening a business that is open to the public (say, a store, restaurant, day-care center, dry cleaner), be very specific and detailed in this section. For example, if your sister has bought a building in the business district on Main Street and has offered you the first-floor retail space for free, make a big deal of it. It shows lots of benefits to investors—great location and free rent.

Products/Services Offered

This is just an outline of what you will be selling. If you plan to open a hair salon, be very specific about all the planned services, from cutting, coloring, and perms to manicures, pedicures, and waxing. Keep it simple—bulleted points are fine—because you will be going into more depth later.

Investors

List anybody and everybody you are borrowing money from for your business. Also include the terms, whether it's a loan or an investment. If Aunt Sue invested $5,000 in your future Pilates studio in exchange for free classes, write that down.

Market Analysis

You market analysis is the place to demonstrate how much you know about your new venture. You know what is out there, what needs to be out there, and what you are going to bring to the table. Summarize your market research and describe your customers. This is where it really pays to do the research. Pound the pavement a little. Call your local library and make an appointment with the business librarian (found in large libraries, they are generally women and love to help); interview other business owners in the area; talk to people in your industry; read trade magazines and newspapers; and join your local chamber of commerce.

The Women's Business Center suggests including the following sections in the "Market Analysis."

Overview of Your Industry

If you are opening a women's shoe store (wouldn't that be fun!), then you want to include an overview of the shoe industry, with information on historic growth rate, trends, the business cycle, and the industry's general outlook.

Target Market

Your customer base, without whom you can not exist. Start with the biggest and most obvious market and dissect it down, smaller and smaller. If you want to open a wicker furniture store in Cape Cod, Massachusetts, start with the broad category of local homeowners as your customers. Then indicate you intend to expand your customer base to first-time homeowners, interior decorators, and vacation homeowners. Based on your market research, outline the needs of these customers, size of the market, number of customers available to you, levels of pricing based on what your customers will pay, and media you will use to reach them. The Women's Business Center recommends that you not forget the purchasing cycle of your potential customers. Or in girl-speak, who has the final say when it comes to buying your product or service? If you are launching a children's toy store, your target demographic isn't the kids but rather the parents, who are paying for the toys. And their purchasing cycle may include bumps around the holidays and dips during the dead of winter.

Competitive Analysis

Focus your energy on the direct competition. If you're going to be selling white T-shirts and there's a Gap down the street, make sure you illustrate how your T-shirts can compete and how your customer will differ from theirs. Perhaps there are three boutique clothing stores in your area that would be your competitors. Go into these stores, buy their products, look at their decor, talk to their staff, check on their prices, and then outline how your store will compete with these establishments. If there are no real differences between your concept and the competition's, you should rethink your concept.

Rules and Regulations

This would include information such as licenses, permits, structural regulations (for example, many public places must provide wheelchair access), and any other legal or government requirements that need to be addressed. Potential investors need this information, because if your business plan outlines, let's say, a bar concept and there are no liquor licenses available, you will be out of business before you've opened the door. Outline this information right in the beginning, because most permits and licenses take time to apply for and be processed, and there's more red tape and bureaucracy to wade through than you can possibly imagine.

Company Description

Explain your business and how it will be successful. Play up your ability to meet your customers' needs and exceed their expectations; sing the praises of your team and how they're more skilled than your competitor's. Illustrate your competitive advantage in this section. If you are planning to open a bakery in your hometown and your mother, a graduate of a prestigious culinary academy, has agreed to come and work with you, that's a competitive advantage.

Organization and Management

Start with an organizational chart (think family tree) with you at the top, branching down into managers and support staff. Add notes next to titles about what the individual job responsibilities will be. Since you are just launching your business, it might be just you, or you and a partner, for a while. It is important for you and your potential investors that you outline who is controlling and managing the company. If you are starting a cleaning business with your best friend, then outline with names who orders supplies, hires staff, cleans houses and/or businesses, does bookkeeping, heads up marketing efforts. These roles are not set in stone; over time they should evolve and then you can update the plan. Outline your ideal staffing situation, and leave blank the unfilled positions. This exercise should find the holes in your organizational structure.

Legal Structure

In this section state the legal form of ownership (sole proprietor, partnership, corporation, limited liability company [LLC]) and explain the advantages of this structure in your case. As you learned in Chapter 3, you have weighed the advantages and disadvantages of each structure and chosen appropriately. Include the names of the owners and their ownership percentages, as well as their form of ownership (for example, general partner, limited partner).

Management

Since you are just starting out, we are assuming that the management team will consist of you and maybe one other person. If you consider your management team a selling point to potential investors, or you want to outline the responsibilities of the team, then spend some time on this section. If you have someone on board at this point with a fantastic background and track record, by all means dedicate space to describing this team member and emphasize how they are going to benefit your business. If it is just you on the team for the foreseeable future, revisit your strengths in detail.

Board of Directors

If you have incorporated your new business, you have included a board of directors in your filing papers. If you chose to list just you and your business partner, skip this section. If, instead, you spent some time selecting a group of professionals whose expertise you can call on to help your business, by all means highlight their contribution to the success of your business.

Marketing and Sales Strategies

Marketing is all of the methods you are going to employ to reach customers and inspire them to buy your services or products. Before you dive into this section, read Chapter 5, where we offer a variety of interesting and low-cost methods for marketing your business. We also outline the details of a marketing plan, which will help you write at least a good chunk of this section. *Sales* is how you are actually going to sell your products or services. If you are launching a carpet-cleaning business and you are targeting three office buildings on your street as your first customers, then include that market survey here.

Service or Product Line

What is your business selling? If you are a freelance bookkeeper, you are selling your ability to get your clients' finances in order. If you are a caterer, you are offering to take care of your customers' culinary needs for special events. If you are a dress designer, you are selling your ability to create dresses that will make your customers look amazing. In this section, keep in mind that you want to list not specifically what you are selling but rather why people would buy it. From a customer point of view, outline a description of your services or products, making sure to include any patent or copyright information that may be important.

Funding Request

If this plan is for potential investors, here is where you want to outline the funding you will need. Include what your funding needs are and how you are going to use the capital you receive. It is essential for every potential investor, from your Aunt Sue up to a venture capitalist, to know exactly how you are going to spend their money. Include a timeline of how and when you are going to use the money and how long it will last. Potential investors want to know if you are going to be coming back for more soon. If you are going after big money (venture capital money usually runs in the millions), long-range plans must be spelled out in great detail.

Financials

Since you do not have a financial track record to add to your business plan, include the monthly projection forecasts for three years. Use the information we offered earlier in the book to create a monthly and start-up budget (pages 64–65). Then based on your market research and pricing analysis, add your projected sales numbers. Talk to your accountant about this section; maybe she has a client who went through a similar exercise and would be willing to talk to you about this aspect of your plan.

Be prepared to back up your numbers. The market and the competition dictate your prices, so does your research. If you are starting a dog-walking business, your pricing has to reflect what the competition is charging. To charge more than your competitors, you have to offer something additional, like adding an extra half hour to each walk.

Your financials should be more than numbers, though. You will need to explain how you've arrived at the numbers. In the dog-walking scenario, explain that your daily sales projection of $288 is generated from an initial plan to walk twelve dogs a day, twice a day, for $12 per walk.

After you've outlined your start-up costs (the beauty of the dog-walking scenario is that start-up is low; a little neighborhood leafleting and love for dogs is all you need to start) or your initial capital outlay, you need to address your monthly costs. Your costs will be either fixed (occurring on a regular basis) or variable (as in those untimely expenditures that you often can't predict). Some of the more common fixed costs include: payroll, insurance, rent, loan payments, advertising/promotions, legal/accounting/IT services, local travel, supplies, taxes, utilities, and dues and subscriptions. Variable costs include the things that just come up—repairs and equipment replacement, for example.

Your business plan should include a three-year financial projection that includes start-up expenses, a balance sheet, and a cash-flow statement. Year one should be outlined monthly, and years two and three, quarterly. Sample spreadsheets (where all you have to do is plunk in the numbers) are available with the Microsoft Business Plan template that we recommend checking out.

Since having realistic numbers and detailed explanations are the keys to securing funding, get help. A great place to start is SCORE: Counselors to America's Small Business (*www.score.org*). Also check out the Finance Center at the Women's Business Center web site (*www.onlinewbc.gov*).

Wrapping Up

Don't stress! There are many people out there willing to help a girl with a good idea, but you must know that a great business plan will take time to research and write. Since looking at this list of sections can be overwhelming, try to schedule a couple of hours a day to work on the plan. If you are not financially ready to launch your business but loathe your current job, plan time on the weekends to chip away at your business plan. Once you have the first draft of the plan, check with the SBA or SCORE and get feedback. Keep in mind that your business plan is a working and living document. You'll be writing initially to secure financing. As your business develops, check in and revisit your financial projections. Take it from us, it's a big help to have begun the business planning process from day one.

FANTASTIC FEMALE ARTISTS

Download some or all of the music by these incredible women to get you through writing the business plan. A little musical inspiration goes a long way.

Fergie and the Black Eyed Peas
"I Gotta Feeling"

Beyoncé
"Single Ladies (Put a Ring on It)"

Alicia Keyes
We're partial to her debut album, *The Diary of Alicia Keyes*.

Madonna
We like *Ray of Light*, but a greatest hits collection is a good call too.

Adele
Her Grammy-winning *Chasing Pavements*

Chrissie Hynde and the Pretenders
The ultimate woman in rock'n'roll. Still.

Chaka Khan
"Tell Me Something Good"

Taylor Swift
"Fearless"

Mary J. Blige
"No More Drama"

Mariah Carey
"The Emancipation of Mimi"

Aretha Franklin
"Soul Queen"

---

girl talk	**Chris Wolfer, President and Cofounder** Construction Information Systems

What should go in a business plan and why do I need to write one? Two questions asked by Chris Wolfer, president and cofounder of Construction Information Systems (an Internet-based leads service for the construction industry), when queries from the investment community forced her to create a business plan three years after launching her business.

When did you write your first business plan? And how did you get it started?
We actually didn't write our first real business plan until three years after we started the company. For free guidance, we went

to the New Jersey Small Business Development Center at Rutgers University. (To find out about small business development centers in your area, log on to *www.sba.gov/sbdc* or visit the online Women's Business Center at *www.onlinewbc.gov*). They will evaluate your company development to see if you have potential and a solid business model. If you qualify, they hire a consultant to work with you to put together a very professional business plan. We qualified and got fifteen hours of consulting. Our consultant actually encouraged us to go back and request more hours so we could do the marketing plan too.

Have you revised it since then?
Twice, actually. We learned enough about the process to be able to revise the plans ourselves, and we considered soliciting investment twice. Business plans in the formal way that they do them at the SBD are really good for investors. They force you to do market surveys if you are thinking about expanding in a new direction, and they spend a lot of time on the narrative.

Is there an alternative to a business plan?
Yes, simple goal setting. Every year I set short- and long-term goals for each department in an outline form. I then convene my management team, assign priorities, and figure out how much it will cost to reach our goals. We then make our decisions based on cash-flow and budget projections. I then transcribe our goals into my strategic planning calendar, which syncs to my phone. And here's the critical part that I think most people actually miss: Every quarter I force (and it really is force) my management team to sit with me and go through all of our goals. We make adjustments and analyze our progress. Typically we'll have three categories: "things that we accomplished," "what didn't happen and why," and "postponed or off the table." In June (we operate on a calendar year) I revise

our budgets and forecast out another six months. We are always working from a year's worth of numbers.

What process do you use for setting financial goals?
At this point, it's all history. Of course it's hard when starting up. When we first started, we got as much of our information from the competitors as we could. You'd be surprised how much information people put on their web sites. We are purposefully vague on our site—our business is really competitive. We actually have so much sales history that we plan to spend 95 percent of our projected sales. We focus on aggressive growth and are constantly investing back into the company. When you're first starting, leave a larger margin for error.

Did you create the plan for in-house operations or to seek outside funding?
We always made the plan for in-house use, but we kept getting requests from people who wanted to invest in the company. We also checked out venture capital funding through the New Jersey Entrepreneurs Fund. We attended some seminars and did some networking. It was a good way to meet people and see how other people were doing it. In the end, we never pursued equity funding because we realized we could fund appropriate growth ourselves. It wasn't worth it to us to give up the control of the company. We are building the company for our future, not to sell.

How long did it take to write the initial plan, and was it worth the effort?
It took a long time, probably between twenty and thirty hours. It was hard to dedicate that much time away from the day-to-day running of the business. If you aren't looking for outside investment, I think a formal business plan is a total waste of time. Do regular budgets, marketing plans, goal setting, and follow-up

instead. Formal business plans are very time-consuming and rarely put to good use.

What advice do you have for women small business owners who are sitting down to write their business plan for the first time?

Make it easy, not overwhelming. Focus on the budgets, goal setting, and marketing. Also make sure you do concentrated market research and a thorough competitive analysis.

Do you have any favorite resources to improve your business skills?

I am a big advocate of seminars and books on tape. I try out different ones: time management, employee management and motivation, sales tactics. It's pretty easy to get away for a day or pop a tape in when you're out in your car. I'm also a fan of the *Harvard Business Review*. It doesn't come out too often, so it's not overwhelming. It targets senior management and offers many creative ways of handling all sorts of challenges. It's also inspiring. The case studies are good reads, and they energize me. I can't say that I've encountered any general business books worth the read.

How do you keep CIS on track and growing?

Here's the biggest challenge to running your business: Doing all of the things that you have to do when you start out. It's hard to stay focused on moving the company forward when you're dealing with the day-to-day operations. Who can think about three years down the road when the garbage is overflowing and you're the only one to take it out? Force yourself to stay focused on the bigger picture. Schedule time to do your planning, and network within your industry. Don't lose sight of the fact that sales drive the entire company, and you've always got to be selling.

Can you tell us about CIS's growth?

We started with only one employee and lots of help from friends and family. The two of us (and many of our helpers) didn't take any money out of the company for the first couple of years. My partner actually waited four years. I was putting in about twenty percent of the money I earned bartending during the first two years. We made a critical error in judgment when we first started, by overestimating the quality of our competitor's reports. As a result, we focused on producing the highest quality product we could before we were willing to sell it. In other words, we dragged our feet about selling because we were afraid it wasn't good enough. In hindsight, we put ourselves at great risk of losing the entire operation, because we weren't growing fast enough. Luckily, it didn't play out that way.

We didn't actually start making progress until two years in, when we hired a salesperson, and then we more than doubled the number of clients that year. We've been growing at a steady rate ever since. We now have almost a thousand clients and thirty-five employees.

Anything you would like to add?

Three things:

(1) I don't think we could have survived the first four years without tremendous help from family, friends, and business acquaintances. I was shocked at how much the other businesses in our office complex were willing to do for us, often for free. We knew we would never be able to pay it back, so I decided to pay it forward. We let other people use our office space at no cost when it's available. I have also developed a strong sense of the importance of supporting local merchants. That's the real reason I go to the deli upstairs—he's not nearly as good as the guy down the road.

(2) Get out there. The more you network in your industry, the more successful you'll be. Don't be afraid to tell people who you are and what you do.

(3) Surround yourself with positive-thinking people and people who are going through similar entrepreneurial experiences. Talk to them. Share your challenges and accomplishments. Stay away from the naysayers. They just bring you down, and there's no time to be brought down when you're starting your own business.

5

Sell It, Sister!
Getting Your Name and Product "Out There"

After telling your friends, dry cleaner, and manicurist that you are starting a new business, it's time to generate a customer base. Your job is to create and follow a cohesive and realistic marketing plan. In this chapter we discuss the marketing options available to you, including advertising, public relations, newsletters, and events, along with the importance of establishing a corporate identity. We also offer tips for hiring and working with professionals and companies who will execute promotional efforts, including designers, printers, writers, advertising agencies, and public relations firms.

First Things First: The Name Game

Naming your business is one of the most important decisions you will make. The name you choose has to appeal to your customers, represent the services or products you offer, and be legally available. Before you fall too in love with a name, do a search for the URL and make sure your lawyer or accountant runs a check for you with the city, state, and federal agencies to confirm that no one else has claimed it before you.

Carrie Herrington, owner of Farmhouse and Farmhouse Flowers, launched her furniture and flower shops under a different name. Her lawyer had checked with the state and confirmed that it was available. Carrie forged ahead, registed her domain name, had signs made, and printed letterhead and business cards. Everything was moving along, until she received a letter from a furniture business in another state informing her that they owned the name and that according to the law, she couldn't use it. "When my lawyer registered my company, they did a state search, not a national search. Because there are lots of businesses with the same name in the same line of work, typically there isn't a conflict." However, since so many businesses are launching web sites that are accessible to everyone, anywhere, companies won't share names.

Carrie Herrington recommends that you "think of your company as growing and do a national search. I went into it thinking I had a small store and that I would stay that way. But you have to look ahead and consider that maybe one day you want to expand and open in other states. You need to prepare for growth." And preparing for growth begins with choosing a name that you can take with you.

When choosing a name, make sure that it is timeless and not too trendy; it clearly represents you and your business; it will work as a logo (not too many words); and most of all—that you like it. Your company's name is the anchor theme that runs through your entire business. Our original name, YC Public Relations, worked for us only for about two years, and then we realized that we'd chosen a name that didn't accurately represent our services. So thousands of dollars later (we had to pay a designer for a new logo and reprint all of our letterhead), we are finally happy with YC Media. Remember, even if you've verified that the name is available, run it by your professional and personal circle to get feedback. Maybe it is available for a reason.

As soon as you choose a name, and your accountant or attorney registers it, go to an on-line business site that offers domain names, such as *register.com* or *networksolutions.com*, and register it. Make sure you register for all possible versions of your company name and have your web designer "point" all of the domains to your main site. When we searched for *www.girlsguide.com*, it had already been taken, so we chose *www.girlsguidetobusiness.com*, a long URL, but one that accurately reflects our point of difference in the marketplace. And then we embarked on registering all of the variations for it, so there is never any confusion. When we launched our fourth book, *Happy at Work, Happy at Home: The Girl's Guide to Working Motherhood*, we changed our URL to *www.happyatworkhappyathome.com*, but it still points to our main site, eliminating confusion for our readers and saving a little money on the migration of the site from one place to another. Make sure you ask lots of questions of your web consultant—we've learned the hard way that they rarely offer the simplest or most inexpensive fix—they want to build fancy solutions that are rarely necessary and always too expensive.

Sexy or Simple: Creating Your Corporate Identity

Once you have the name, it's time to start thinking about your corporate identity. A corporate identity is the "look" you create for your business that appears on everything from your logo to your letterhead. The key to choosing the right image for your company is to always keep yourself and your customer in mind, because while it has to appeal to you, it also has to appeal to your potential customers. Rachel Berliner, cofounder and co-owner of Amy's Kitchen, an organic and vegetarian frozen food company, shares that when she and her husband were working with a designer to come up with an identity, they had some challenges: "Since Amy's is a company that is really an extension of who we are, we wanted something that both appealed to us personally and also popped out on the store shelves. And since we had zero marketing budget in the beginning, our packaging had to do a lot for us." They went with a simple signature for the logo, used along with bright, bold colors for the product names and descriptions. The beautiful colors and great food shots effectively pop Amy's soups, pizzas, and entrées off the shelves.

The identity should reflect the kind of business you own. Susi Oberhelman, founder of SVO Graphic Design, says, "Think about what you want to convey with your logo. Everything from strength and whimsy to fun and intelligence can all be expressed. You just have to decide what you want people to think and feel when they see it." If you are launching a vintage clothing store, you may want to use clothes, attics, trunks, or other images that represent this theme on your logo, labels, and bags.

Starbucks is a company that has created a complete, unified, instantly recognizable corporate identity and used it on everything from their coffee cups, bags of beans, napkins, gift packaging, to all of those seasonal point-of-sale items you riffle through while waiting at the counter for your latte. Many think they have taken it too far, but they are a great example of a company taking every opportunity available to stick their corporate identity under your nose. Whatever "look" you decide on, you want to use it with everything that goes out from your business, from shipping labels to envelopes. You should also personalize forms such as invoices and contracts with your logo.

GOLDEN ARCHES: OUR FIVE FAVORITE LOGOS

Nike
This logo is subtle, classic, timeless, and cool. Supported by years of strong advertising campaigns, at this point it says "healthy lifestyle."

Starbucks
Since the company puts their green mermaid on everything from cups to napkins, consumers now associate the image with a cup of coffee. Brilliant.

Target
This company has had several years of incredibly successful ad campaigns, and their cherry red bull's-eye is always front and center. At this point, the stand-alone image represents all things hip and cheap.

Apple
This logo has been around for years, but since the company changes the color of the logo, in concert with its new products, it is always up-to-date.

Chanel
The interlocking Cs in a clean, clear font is a classic example of "less is more."

TEN TIPS FOR CHOOSING A LOGO

1. Love it or lose it

You will be looking at this logo every day for the foreseeable future, so pick something you will like tomorrow, next year, and on the tenth anniversary of your business.

2. Make sure the dress fits the occasion

Your logo—it gives people the first impression they will have of you and your business, so make sure it reflects your identity, tone, and service. One designer came to us with a charming graphic for our business—an old-fashioned tandem bicycle. We got the concept—there are two of us. It looked great and classy, but the image said nothing about our public relations business. Had we been opening an antiques store, it would have been ideal.

3. Colors are key

Choose colors (black and white count) that reflect your corporate identity and appeal to your potential customers and clients.

4. Perfect big or small

Your logo may be reduced, enlarged, colorized, or printed in black and white over the course of your business, so make sure the logo you pick will look perfect in any incarnation.

5. Don't choose the wrong icon

This is a business decision. Don't fall in love with a logo that you know is not right for the services or products you are selling.

6. Get feedback

Show your logo to respected friends, family members, and acquaintances. If they don't respond positively, ask them why. Ask what the logo "says" to them. If it's what you want people to say about your company, you could be on the right track.

7. Versatility is key

Your logo must look good on a variety of promotional materials, including letterhead, business cards, signs, stickers, magnets, and especially a web site, so make sure it is versatile. Also be sure it will show up when e-mailed or photocopied. A designer created a really hip logo for a friend's freelance writing business, however, when it was reproduced, the logo, along with all of the important contact information, disappeared.

8. You might not need a logo

If you are opening a law practice or offering bookkeeping services on the weekend, then save money and just get a generic business card and letterhead with your contact information on it.

9. Use professionals

While the guy at the local copy store may seem really enthusiastic about creating a logo for you, invest in hiring a professional graphic designer with a track record. Ask to see their portfolio or check out their web site for samples.

10. This isn't going to be cheap

Designing a great logo and identity package is worth the investment. Shop around for designers, printers, and paper, but make sure you go with the best option. If you have a limited printing budget, do things in stages and just get business cards and letterhead done right away.

Marketing: What Is It?

Marketing is everything and anything you do to get your company in front of potential clients and customers. Marketing—digital and traditional—is an umbrella; all of your activities that will generate customers fall under that umbrella. When starting your business, outline a marketing plan and then prioritize your efforts. Sherry Treco-Jones, presi-

dent of Treco-Jones Public Relations, Inc., says, "The first step is to outline a marketing plan with respect to your goals and assign budget estimates to each activity (networking, luncheons, direct mail, print
advertising, business cards/logo/letterhead, web site, etc.)." But keep in
mind that you want a diverse selection of marketing outreach. Nancy
Forman, owner of Language Liaison, Inc., recommends not putting all
of your eggs in one basket: "I put one hundred percent of my budget into
my web site, which almost caused my business to go bankrupt when I
had problems with it."

Based on the needs of most small businesses, the items under your
marketing umbrella could include:

Promotional Pieces (business cards, letterhead, brochures)

Web Sites

Promotions

Public Relations

Advertising

Speaking Engagements

Special Events and Sponsorships

Networking

Social Networking

I Have a Web Site, Therefore I Am

Doing business on the web has changed dramatically since the original
edition of *The Girl's Guide to Starting Your Own Business* was first published. Web sites used to be a luxury; now they are an absolutely critical representation of your business—even if they are nothing more than
one page of information. You can put up a blog or even a fully function-
ing site in less than an hour.

Our friends at Cool Hunting (*www.coolhunting.com*) explain: The most important thing is to be out there. A simple page with some text on it will help people find you and also get your name registered with search engines. It's much more important to be on-line in a small way than to stress about having the biggest, best, fanciest presence. Just get out there and evolve as you can.

You should consider all of the many free tools available to you: Twitter, Facebook, and any of the many blogging platforms (Blogger, Type-Pad, and WordPress, for example) are good places to start. If you are selling things, there are many free e-commerce platforms available, and just about every computer company or web host offers free easy-to-build web site platforms. You should also make sure details are current on sites like Yelp, Citysearch, Google Maps, and others if you have a physical presence.

Web Design

Before jumping in with an expensive designer, give some thought to what you are using your site for, because that will determine what you put there. If you open a law firm, you probably just want to use the web site to take the place of expensive printed marketing materials. Include your bio, a firm profile, a page about your specific practice, and contact information. If you open a retail shop that specializes in folk art, you are probably using the web site to introduce new customers to your store and to inspire both new and returning customers to buy your products. In that case, you want to include a home page, several product pages organized by category (have the products professionally photographed!), the option to order on-line, and contact information. You might also include a brief "Folk Art 101" or links to folk art museums to keep people engaged.

Once you know what you want to include on your web site, the time has come for you to write the materials, get the products (or you) photographed, and start compiling links if you are going to have any. When writing your home page, remember that you are selling something, so you want to use language that will inspire your customer to buy something or contact you. Think along the lines of "we provide excellent service" rather than "we know accounting." If you are hiring a writer, make sure she has the time and the commitment to get your project done. If you are having photographs taken, do some on-line research and check out how successful competitors offer their products. If you like their style, show your photographer exactly the look you are going for. If you are opening a kitchen store and are having a photographer come in to shoot your tabletop items and new roasters, then go on-line and see how Williams-Sonoma and Sur La Table are showcasing their products.

Once the written materials are complete, the photographs are taken, and the logo is finished, it's time to design the site. You can either create it yourself using a program such as Microsoft FrontPage, an on-line template (*http://freesitetemplates.com*), or hire a professional. If you are like us, you will find it easier—albeit more expensive—to work with a professional web designer. By now you know the hiring-consultants drill: See their work, get recommendations, ask for competitive bids, and always check references. Designers may have a flat rate for an agreed-upon number of pages—the ones we spoke to charged between two and five hundred dollars for five easy pages—and some charge by the hour.

If you work with a designer, you will also be paying her by the hour to update your site. This can add up, so if you are on a limited budget—and who isn't—keep this in mind when designing your site. Consider including timeless information there, maybe just your contact information and a general information page about you and your business.

Do it right the first time. Don't launch a site you are not 100 percent pleased with just to get something up there. Remember, your web site will be the first introduction many potential clients have to your company, so it must be a good representation of your business. We made the mistake of rushing our company's web site our first time and had to spend additional money to fix it.

The design of the web site should reflect your corporate identity, be easy to navigate and organized logically, offer reasons for someone to spend time there and return, minimize the clicks (too many clicks and a customer might decide not to buy), and look great. An accountant might want to offer the latest tax information on her site, or a wedding planner could put up photos of a recent job, articles about the current wedding trends, or photographs of seasonal bouquets.

You Have a Web Site—Now What?

Once you have a web site, you need to purchase a web-hosting service. A web-hosting service is a company that can not only get you up on the web but can offer additional services, such as e-mail accounts (so customers can reach you) and e-commerce capabilities (if you are selling over the web). You can do it yourself, but it is really expensive and complicated. If you are looking for limited services—just the web site hosting without e-mail—then the cost will be very low, and if your needs are more complicated, the cost typically runs about one hundred and fifty dollars a month through *doteasy.com*.

Submitting your site to search engines such as *google.com* or *yahoo.com* is the first step. To ensure that your web site will be listed in search engines you have to submit them yourself (or your designer can do this for you) by logging on to *addme.com* or *siteadd.com*. It is typically free, but make sure you submit your web site name every few months and optimize it by submitting it with key words. For instance, if you open a florist shop in Keene, New Hampshire, then submit your location plus the key words *flowers, florist, floral arrangements, floral delivery, flower arrangements, flower delivery,* and *bouquets*. This way if someone types in *Keene flower arrangements*, your business will pop up.

When it comes to directly marketing your web site, Sylvia Tooker, owner of Bear Data Services, an Internet consulting and design business, advises entrepreneurs to, "first, think of the people you want to sell to off-line. Then take it to the next step and think of how you could reach them on-line. You should ask yourself, what are my customer's interests? What are they searching for on-line?"

Linking your web site to complementary sites is also important. If you launch a yoga studio in upstate New York, you may want to research the opportunities for linking your site to the sites of the local chamber of commerce, health clubs in your area, or local athletic stores.

For those of you who are launching a web site business and your money will be made from selling banner ads and not from customers, Tara Paterson, founder and owner of *www.justformom.com*, a web site dedicated to offering resources and networking opportunities for moms, suggests that "first and foremost you have to build relationships. You can't do it any other way. Join networking groups such as Business Networking International and the local chamber of commerce."

Last, but most important, remember to add your web site address to your letterhead, business cards, and everything else you send out from your business. Also set up an e-mail address from your site so that you will begin to promote its existence through your communication efforts.

Referral Arrangements

Since your marketing budget will be limited, look for other complementary small businesses to set up referral arrangements. If you are opening a catering business, find the best florists in town and offer to recommend them to your clients in exchange for the same courtesy. If starting a photography business, contact local event planners about promoting one another's businesses to clients. A public relations business may want to enlist a marketing consultant as a referral partner. Aligning yourself with another small business of quality can enhance your corporate identity, build word-of-mouth business, and save on precious marketing dollars.

Promotions 101:
Giveaways, Coupons, and Sales

A promotion is a marketing tool to "promote" something to your clients. It can be anything from a winter sale to a free yoga class. Running promotions too frequently can reek of desperation. Run a promotion when you first open your business to attract customers, hang your launch advertising campaign on, and help generate coverage in the local media. Run a promotion if your business introduces a new service or product. When we decided to offer media-training services to our clients, we offered a reduced rate for the first session. Maybe you could partner with another local business that complements yours and run a co-promotion—your restaurant offers a free dessert to those coming in after seeing a movie at the local theater in exchange for the movie house's advertising the restaurant. Copromotions are a nice way to save money, and having the right partner can add to your brand image. Susan Kirshenbaum, founder of Kirshenbaum Communications, suggests, "Run offers that can be delivered upon when you are not busy—tax season offers, summer specials, year-end discounts, free one-hour consultations on a new service—and plan ahead to keep the work flow steady."

Make sure it is a promotion that:

Appeals directly to your target customers.

Represents you and your business well.

Does not come off as a desperate move.

Runs infrequently.

Has a clear start and end date.

Public Relations Primer: What Is a Press Release, Exactly?

With advertising, you pay a newspaper or TV show to promote your business. With public relations, you or your representative works directly with editors, producers, and bloggers to include or feature your company in a story. The results can be much more effective than an ad because with a PR placement, a third party (editor or blogger) has given an unofficial nod to your business. Think about it. If you see an advertisement for a new bed-and-breakfast, you probably don't give it a second thought. But if you read about how fabulous and romantic the bed-and-breakfast is in *USA Today*, chances are you will remember it because a national newspaper acknowledged and wrote about it.

Even if you are new to the concept of public relations, you have unknowingly been seeing the results of the efforts of public relations representatives on a daily basis. The chef you caught this morning on your local news, shown demonstrating the best way to roast a turkey, was probably placed there by public relations folks who specialize in food clients (like us!). The story you read about Brad Pitt showing up at a screening for a new independent film was placed by the public relations representative of the film's distribution company. The interview with a bestselling mystery writer on your favorite radio station was set up by the publicist for her publishing company. There are publicists in every industry, and the good ones get their clients coverage on the television shows, magazines, newspapers, radio shows, and the web sites that reach their customer base.

WHAT DO WE MEAN BY THE "RIGHT" TELEVISION SHOWS, MAGAZINES, NEWSPAPERS, RADIO SHOWS, AND WEB SITES? At any point in the process of launching a business, you should have a clear idea of who your potential customers are. They may be young women, grandparents, college students, single men. You have a demographic in mind when you create your business concept, and when it comes to public relations, you want to think of what your potential customers are watching, reading, and listening to. A public relations professional, once hired to represent you, will work to place stories about your company or set up interviews with you in these media outlets.

When we were hired by Nudo, a UK–based company that offers an "Adopt an Olive Tree in Italy" gift, we targeted the top foodie web sites and blogs for coverage. We wanted an on-line campaign because the easiest way to adopt the tree was on-line. We secured coverage on *www.marthastewart.com*, *www.yumsugar.com*, *www.apartmenttherapy .com*, and *www.coolhunting.com*. By placements on just those four sites, Nudo was able to quadruple their U.S. sales over the previous year.

Our e-mail pitch for Nudo read like this:

> We just started working with **Nudo: Adopt an Olive Tree**, and
> are really excited about both the product and the concept.
> Nudo is a family-run cooperative of olive groves dotted
> around a small hilltop village in the Marche region of Italy,

and they offer the unique chance to own a little piece of the Italian countryside.

Olive growing has become more mechanized in recent years, which has led to both soil erosion and bland, mass-produced oil. Because of this (and recent issues with lax regulations on olive oil origin), eco-conscious food lovers demand olive oil from small-scale, artisanal farmers. With Nudo, they know exactly where their oil comes from; right down to the GPS coordinates! Instead of just buying olive oil, by adopting a tree you can choose a specific olive variety, follow the progress of your tree for one year, support the local Italian family farmer, and (literally) taste the reward of your investment.

Once you adopt a tree from Nudo, you or the gift recipient will receive a personalized adoption certificate and information booklet that describes the tree, four 500-ml tins of first cold press extra-virgin olive oil from the tree in the spring (mid-April), three 250-ml tins of infused extra-virgin olive oil (i.e., lemon, chile, orange) in the fall, and an open invitation to come and visit, hug, or water the tree in person. The adoption and products cost $150.00, making it a thoughtful present or very reasonable group gift.

Nudo has just recently begun shipping efforts in the United States, and I'd love to send you a sample adoption kit with olive oil for you to try yourself. Let me know if you would like any additional info or images as well.

HOW DO THEY DO IT? Every public relations representative has a style for getting press placements. We approach journalists with story ideas that we know are suitable only for their outlet. Some agencies hit everybody up with the same story idea, hoping that something will stick. Some public relations agencies have built their companies on celebrity clients, so that journalists call them when looking for a story about stars. When choosing a public relations representative, you want to make sure her style matches yours.

| the word | **Sherry Treco-Jones**
Treco-Jones Public Relations |

On working with a public relations agency:

If a new business owner is inexperienced in public relations, she should seek a good understanding from her consultant or public relations agency of what to expect in her relationship with them and from the anticipated work.

The owner should also have a public relations plan for her business developed and then executed by the agency—and measurable in terms of agreed-upon reasonable results within a specific time frame and budget. The agency should be working on the plan and measuring that work or explaining why there's an alteration or problem if one occurs. If none or only some of this happens, a problem exists.

Sometimes the day-to-day account executive's style does not flow well with the client's style. The business owner shouldn't throw out the baby with the bathwater—only request an account team change. However, if that change is not effective, that's a problem too.

THINGS TO KNOW WHEN HIRING AN AGENCY. Ask to see a client list *before* setting up a meeting. If you are starting a jewelry design business with your own designs and a potential agency shows you a client list that includes all of your competitors, move on. How will the public relations agency pitch stories about you while doing the same for your competitors? If the client list shows your competitors as previous clients and you noticed lots of articles about them in the past, then do some more digging around. Perhaps the agency has fantastic contacts that resulted in many stories about your competitors, but there could have been differences in style that led to ending the relationships. What you want to see on a client list is companies that you have been reading about, companies that you respect, and companies that complement but don't compete with yours. Sherry Treco-Jones tells us that "a company needs to select an agency that not only can do their business but reflects their preferences in an agency (sometimes the result of bad lessons learned). One example may be the need for a high level of attention from the agency's account team. No one wants their account to be at the bottom of the billings rung. Often, this requires a match with the right-sized agency."

GET TO KNOW YOUR PUBLIC RELATIONS CONTACT. In addition to choosing a firm that has a style that reflects your business, you also want a publicist who does the same. When meeting with potential agencies, ask who will be working on your account day to day. With big agencies come big staff, and though you may have met with the owner of the company, she will probably not be the one calling the media on your behalf. So while it is important to feel comfortable with the agency, it's more important to have a good feeling and a strong relationship with your individual contact. Before you sign with an agency, be clear that you want approval over who will be working on your account. We have heard too many stories about entrepreneurs new to hiring agencies who were wooed by the president of an agency in the first meeting, only to find out two weeks later that a college freshman was doing the majority of work on their account. A youngster still in school won't have the contacts necessary to place a story about your business.

WHAT ARE PRESS CLIPS, AND WHY AM I LOOKING AT THEM? Most agencies will pull out stacks of press results for you to sift through during your first meeting with them to impress you with their results. The press clips—especially the bigger placements—should be recent. If the *Time*, *People*, and *Glamour* articles were dated 2000, while the local newspaper articles were dated 2009, perhaps the agency has lost its edge.

ASK FOR REFERENCES. Just as with a job candidate, ask for references from the agency, but do some digging on your own. Call a few of their past clients. Ask others in your business whom they recommend. If you know any journalists who cover your field, ask them if they like working on stories with the agency. You will be surprised how much you can learn about the style of a company.

HOW DO AGENCIES GET PAID? Most public relations agencies work for clients on a monthly retainer. An art gallery owner may hire a public relations firm on a retainer basis to make sure that her new exhibits are always on the radar of local critics. Some agencies work on a per project basis. Then the art gallery owner would hire the public relations firm to promote one show, for example.

While hiring an agency for a short-term project might save you money in the long run, you will need to have more money up front, because many will bill you 50 percent of the total fee upon signature of the contract. The fees range depending on the size of the agency (bigger agencies have more overhead and charge higher prices), the scope of the project (if you want the agency to go after the *Today* show rather than your local noon news, it will cost more), and where you are located (New York City agencies charge more than Kansas City agencies). Fees are usually negotiable, but be clear with the agency from the get-go what your budget is, so that you don't waste each other's time. And don't forget . . . fees are just fees. They don't include expenses, and larger agencies in particular charge for every piece of letterhead, phone call, and rubber band.

CAN YOU DO IT YOURSELF? The answer is yes if your goals are to get your company mentioned in your local media. If that is your only goal, then by all means try it. Reach out to a local reporter and introduce yourself. But before you call or e-mail, you need to have a story idea. If you are announcing that your store is opening, then that is your story. If you have a flower shop and you are carrying a batch of exotic orchids, that's your story.

Once you have the story idea, do some research. Find out who at your local paper covers that beat; confirm the spelling of her name and her title. Send her a press release (we discuss press releases next) or a letter, and give her a week to check back in with you. If you don't hear from her, shoot her an e-mail introducing yourself and asking if the newspaper can use the information you sent her. If your goal is to get national attention or coverage outside of your local area, you might be better off hiring a professional.

FOUR TIPS FOR EFFECTIVE E-MAIL PITCHES

1. Target your pitches. Don't send a mass e-mail to bloggers and editors. Demonstrate that you have read their blog or columns and that you are sending them relevant material that they should read. You don't want to become known for spam.

2. Don't make the HTML formats too fancy. Bloggers and editors hate e-mails that freeze their in-boxes with large photos. Instead let them know in your e-mail that you have photos available to illustrate their stories.

3. Mail-merge programs in Outlook are a good way to customize e-mails and send more than one at a time.

4. Don't bombard editors with e-mails. Give them time to read and respond to you. If they don't respond to two e-mails, then pick up the phone and give them a call.

PR: Press Release 101

A press release answers the basic who, what, when, where, why, and how of a story idea for a reporter or producer. It gives journalists reasons for covering a story as well as information that makes writing the story as easy for them as possible. If you are opening a gourmet take-out store in town, send a press release to the local paper that states who you are and what the business is, when the opening is taking place, and why this is big news. Include your store hours and a menu of items that will be sold. Pay attention to similar articles in your local paper. What information is in there? What makes the story interesting?

The release should ideally be no longer than one page. Busy journalists don't have time to read a six-page release. Since you are sending the release to professionals in the communications field, it should be well written, concise, and most important, grammatically correct. Don't rely on spell-check either. We can't tell you how many journalists have told us that they won't take a release seriously if it is filled with spelling errors. And a few, very bitter, writers keep files of the worst press releases for laughs. Yikes. You don't want to be in that file, so check your grammar, and ask at least two other people to proofread it for clarity and mistakes. The format of a release is fairly standardized. Don't deviate too much or you will come across as unprofessional.

Read the mastheads of your local daily and weekly newspapers, and send the release to the journalists who cover the relevant beat (business). Follow the blogs for a few days so you can craft a relevant pitch. If the release announces the opening of your new business, we recommend sending it to complementary businesses. If you are opening a cheese store, put all of the surrounding wine stores and bakeries on your press release mailing list. If you are opening a children's clothing store, post the release at area schools, day-care centers, and at your local Y.

Our sample press release announces the launch of a new book we worked on. You will notice that we included the who, what, when, where, why, and how in the first few paragraphs of the release. This release was sent to all the on-line and traditional outlets that would consider coverage for the book. We sent the release both by hard copy, with copies of the book, to our top targets, and by e-mail, offering to send review copies to our secondary contacts—saving money on postage and additional review copies.

For immediate release
Please contact: Kimberly Yorio or Aimee Bianca
kim@ycmedia.com or aimee@ycmedia.com
212-609-5009

MICHAEL SYMON'S LIVE TO COOK
Recipes and Techniques to Rock Your Kitchen
By Michael Symon and Michael Ruhlman

"If I can't finish a dish in two pans, I won't do it," says Michael Symon in the introduction to his new book, MICHAEL SYMON'S LIVE TO COOK: *Recipes and Techniques to Rock Your Kitchen* (Clarkson Potter, November 4, 2009; $32.50/hardcover). Not quite the words you'd expect to hear from one of America's most celebrated chefs, but exactly why home cooks across America will be thrilled to have his first cookbook as part of their collection.

Food Network's *Iron Chef America,* *Food & Wine*'s "Best New Chef," and James Beard's "Best Chef, Midwest" are just a few of the accolades that Michael has received over the years; and while Michael can play on the biggest stages in American cooking, he prefers his hometown of Cleveland and the cooking of his heritage, based on recipes beloved by his parents—one of Greek-Italian ancestry, and the other with an Eastern-European background—and the community of his favorite midwestern city.

If you've seen him on Food Network, you know him by his laugh. One look through his cookbook and you'll be hooked on his food. Michael's cookbook is more than a collection of recipes. In LIVE TO COOK, he sets out "to make great food more approachable for home cooks and to do so without dumbing down or simplifying the food or the cooking." The first step is to start shopping better, and he offers some simple guidelines for doing so: buy with the seasons; buy fresh oils and good vinegars (and don't forget you get what you pay for, so spend a little more for quality balsamic, and don't waste it); look for food that is natural and unprocessed. Michael even includes a list of "Five Things You Should Never Buy," which includes skinless, boneless breasts of chicken, lean turkey bacon, butter substitutes, beef tenderloin, and peeled, chopped garlic.

After an essay on salt and demystifying the creation of a balanced dish, he writes, "Without question two of the most critical elements of a dish are fat and acid. The fat is what gives you that great mouth feel and the acidity helps cut through the fat to keep your palate alive and jumping." Michael brings it all together first in a demonstration using one of his signature recipes, *Halibut with Fried Capers, Caramelized Lemon, and Almonds,* and then in more than one hundred of his favorite dishes.

His chapters include: "Starters"; "Soups and Sandwiches"; "Salads"; "Pasta, Gnocchi, and Risotto"; "Charcuterie;" "Pickles"; "Stocks, Sauces, and Condiments"; "Side Dishes"; "Fish"; "Meat"; and "Family Meal" and include recipes ranging from the simplest (*Roasted Dates with Pancetta, Almonds, and Chile*) to the most sophisticated (*Poached Foie Gras Bratwurst*).

In all Michael's dishes, he draws on the flavors of traditional recipes to create exciting dishes. His *"Beef Cheek Pierogi with Wild Mushrooms and Horseradish"* was inspired by the ones that his grandpa made that he grew up eating. Michael's mother's heritage and cooking are never far from his plates, too, as the Mediterranean ingredients show up in dishes such as *Olive Oil Poached Halibut with Fennel, Rosemary, and Garlic*, and of course there are the reimagined Cleveland favorites like *Mac and Cheese with Roasted Chicken, Goat Cheese, and Rosemary*.

While Michael's food may sound complicated, it's quite simple to prepare. *The Olive Oil Poached Halibut* has only six ingredients and takes only fifteen minutes to cook. Pair it with one of his salads or simple side dishes and you've got a delicious, perfectly balanced restaurant-quality meal. Even his famous beef cheek pierogi recipe, which may look daunting, is broken down into steps that can be easily managed on a Sunday afternoon of cooking, plus the pierogi can be frozen and ready to go for a weeknight meal. Or just make the filling and toss it with pasta. It's that good. As are all of the recipes.

Written with award-winning food writer Michael Ruhlman, this book is as fun to read as it is to cook from. With fantastic four-color photography throughout and tons of helpful "Symon Says" tips, MICHAEL SYMON'S LIVE TO COOK is sure to become one of the cookbooks that you actually cook from—for years to come.

ABOUT THE AUTHOR: Michael Symon is an Iron Chef on Food Network's *Iron Chef America*. He is the chef and co-owner of Lola, Lolita, and Bar Symon in Cleveland, Ohio, as well as Roast in Detroit, Michigan. He was named the James Beard Best Chef in the Midwest in 2009. He lives in Cleveland with his wife, Liz, and their three dogs, and he has a four handicap in golf.

Where Do I Advertise?
InStyle or the *Daily Gazette*?

Advertising is a message about your business that you pay to have aired on television, spoken on the radio, or printed in the newspaper, Yellow Pages, newsletters, or on-line. According to Susan Kirshenbaum, founder of Kirshenbaum Communications, "Advertising is expensive, and for it to be effective, it must be repeated frequently: Think carefully about the placement of the ad, size, message, and offer you are making. Know what your audience reads, and find out the circulation and stats of the publication before placing the ad." Since there are so many options with advertising and the costs are so varied (from the very cheap quarter-inch ad in your local paper to the very expensive thirty-second television spot aired during your local news), you need to first ask yourself a few key questions before deciding on your advertising campaign.

What do I have to spend?
First, review your marketing budget. When your business was launched, you were working from a first-year plan. One of the line items in the launch budget was marketing dollars—the money allotted to spend on advertising, public relations, events, and promotions for a full year. Before putting all of it into one expensively produced television spot, ask yourself these next questions.

Who are my customers?
Yes, we are asking you this question again. Your customers will dictate the success or failure of your business venture. You need to know who they are so that you can communicate with them through a targeted marketing plan. If you review your home-delivery business plan and identify your customers as being senior citizens, find out what television programming, magazines, newsletters, and newspaper columns are geared toward this demographic. These media outlets will be the places where you should advertise.

Where are my customers?

Before you decide to advertise in any medium, make sure your customers are reading it, watching it, or listening to it. If you launched a pizza place in a college town, buying time on the college station is a better bet than on the local NPR station. And rather than advertise in the local paper, take out a print ad in the college paper or in the programs handed out at concerts and games.

On-line banner ads are another option. If the college paper has an on-line version, buy a banner ad that runs with your print ad. Think about how many times you have Googled a local movie theater, dry cleaner, or hairdresser. In the media kits that advertising reps work from—which include ad rates, special-section opportunities, promotional tie-in opportunities—there is a sheet that breaks down their viewers' and readers' demographics by sex, age, and income so you can see if your customers match up to theirs.

What am I advertising?

So now that you know where to advertise to reach your customers and you know how much you have to spend, ask yourself why you are advertising. Great reasons to advertise are business openings, sales and promotions, special event announcements, and anniversaries. If your marketing budget is small, there might be marketing avenues other than advertising, but if you do have the resources, make sure you have something to advertise.

Is my business the kind to advertise?

Even if you have the money in your marketing budget to advertise, some businesses don't really benefit from advertising. For instance, if you launch a high-end restaurant, it usually isn't a good idea to advertise beyond a listing in the Yellow Pages and one or two ads to announce the opening. Since most high-end restaurants resort to advertising only if they are slow, it comes across as desperate. If you have questions about whether your business would benefit, look at your competitors. Are they advertising? Where and how often? What are they advertising? This will help give you some idea of what they are spending on ads, and if they have been in business awhile, then it is probably working for them.

Is it worth it?

Tracking the effectiveness of advertising can be a tricky endeavor, but it's necessary. Whenever you have been asked by a business, "How did you hear about us?" they are trying to find out if advertising is working for them and, more specifically, what kind. Methods of tracking effectiveness can be customer-comment cards, a questionnaire on your web site, redeemable coupons, and then of course you can ask customers point blank, "Did you see my ad this weekend in the *Gazette*?" If you advertise a sale on the radio and the store is flooded with customers afterward, then you know the ad worked. The best way to gauge whether an ad campaign is working is to pay attention to the ebb and flow of the business, communicate with customers, and track exactly what you are advertising and when it appears.

Do I need an advertising agency?

If you are launching a national business or product and you have the budget to place ads in expensive media outlets like monthly magazines (*Cosmopolitan*, *House Beautiful*), national television, and newspapers on the scale of the *Boston Globe*, you may want to consider hiring an advertising agency. They will work with you to create a campaign, design the ads, and work with the media outlets to get you a good deal. For instance, if you are opening an upscale furniture store in a town populated by New York City weekenders, it might be a great idea to advertise in *Town & Country* and the *New York Times*. Since these are very expensive places to advertise, you don't want to risk running a less-than-perfect ad, nor do you want to overpay. In this case, we would recommend using an advertising agency.

However, if you are opening a children's clothing store on a limited marketing budget and are looking to advertise the opening only in the local paper, then forget the advertising agency—do it yourself! Most newspapers—large and small—offer creative services to advertisers. For a nominal fee the creative team at your paper can design the ad and write the copy. Most radio stations will also offer production services for advertising spots, as will local television stations. Remember, they want you to place an ad with them, so they will make it as easy as possible.

| the word | **Susan Kirshenbaum**
Kirshenbaum Communications |

On hiring an advertising agency:

Get recommendations and referrals from business associates based on what you are looking for in terms of budget and your target audience.

Go on-line and do research in your area and check in with professional associations.

Call potential agencies—make sure you include agencies with different capabilities—and ask them to send you an information packet.

Then interview those that fit your criteria. You want to look for an agency that has expertise in your business, smart account people who you like and trust, an understanding of your budget and knows how to get the most bang for your buck—and they show you excellent samples of their campaigns that have brought their clients desired results. The final step—call their references.

Things to Know When Hiring an Agency

If you have the budget to work with an agency, there are a few ways to pick the right one for your business. Ask for a client list to get an idea of the range of clients the agency has worked with. If you are a small business (and we are assuming at this point that you are), look for small agencies that specialize in what you do. If the agency you are interviewing has worked with McDonald's, Barnes & Noble, and Target, you might not be able to afford them and they might not know what to do with your monogramming business.

Look at their web site. You want to see a wide variety of styles represented. If they tailor campaigns to individual clients, the ads will look very different and that is what you want. Ads need to pop off the page or out of the television, and they won't if they look like all of the others.

You want to be specific with the agency about what you need from them. Are you looking for a one-off print ad to announce the launch? Are you looking for a digital campaign that you can use several times throughout the year? Are you looking for television and radio advertisements as well? Be clear with them, because your next step is to ask for a quote, and they can't give a quote if they don't know what you need.

Tell them exactly what your business is and who you are trying to reach with advertising. You want the ad to appeal to you, but more important, to your potential customers as well. And you want it to fit your budget. So tell them exactly how much you have to spend on the creation of the ad.

E-mail Blasts

The most cost-effective way to reach customers is by e-mail. But before you begin sending notes through the Internet, think about what you want to say and why your e-mail will be different from the spam everyone is inundated with every day. Consider working with your web designer to create something visually compelling. The text should be easy to read and the sales pitch available in the subject line. If you run a yoga studio and want to announce new hours, the subject line on the e-mail should read, "SUNLIGHT YOGA STUDIO OFFERS NEW HOURS," so your customers will know exactly what they get when they open it.

Capturing the e-mails of the people who visit your web site is an important tool in your marketing arsenal. If you do, then you can create a community for your product or service that you will be able to communicate with easily and inexpensively. When we launched the *Happy at Work, Happy at Home* book, we signed up with a self-service direct marketing company, VerticalResponse (*www.verticalresponse.com*), so we could easily send all of our big news to our entire list.

Speaking Engagements

Talking to an audience of potential new customers or clients about your business is a gold mine. So how can you set this up? Look around you. Are there complementary businesses that might be interested in having you come in and speak to their customers about your area of expertise? If you opened a restaurant, would a neighboring kitchen appliance store like you to come in and do a cooking demonstration for their customers? If you opened a health club, would a local sporting goods store like you to come in and do a lecture on fitness? Is there a college near you? If so, talk to the business department about you guest-lecturing students on entrepreneurship. Keep your eyes and ears open; opportunities for public speaking are everywhere.

---

the word	**Sharyn Yorio, FSMPS** Sustainable Marketing

Sharyn Yorio, a marketing consultant specializing in working with architects and engineers, is currently a Fellow and has been a member of the Society for Marketing Professional Services (*www.smps.org*) for more than twenty years.

Sharyn is a past president of the SMPS New York chapter and shared with us her tips for maximizing the benefit of membership in a professional organization.

TEN TIPS FOR ADVANCEMENT THROUGH A PROFESSIONAL ASSOCIATION

1. Attend functions regularly. The best way to start building your network is by attending monthly meetings and programs. Over time your network will grow exponentially as the people you meet introduce you to their colleagues.

2. Join a committee. Working side by side with your colleagues on a professional project is one of the best ways to get to know people. Working together to advance a cause or promote your profession is both a learning and bonding experience.

3. Chair a committee. Volunteering for leadership roles serves two purposes. First, it gives you greater visibility. Second, and most important, it builds leadership skills.

4. Write articles. Getting published is a great way to establish yourself as an authority in your field and a spokesperson for your profession.

5. Volunteer to speak. Acting as a moderator or putting together a program on a topic of interest to the membership is an ideal way to get in front of people and make a direct impression.

6. Attend the national conference. If your field has one, make sure you attend the conference. If developing a national network is your goal, this is the place to start. In addition to the learning sessions, networking with your peers on a national level is the best reason to attend.

7. Get on the board of directors or board of advisers. Taking on a leadership role at this level maximizes your visibility and results in real exposure for you and your firm. From a board position, you have genuine influence in decisions that impact the organization and your profession.

8. Submit yourself or your firm for an award. Most professional associations have award programs. While winning an award in itself is gratifying, the free publicity that comes with winning an award is a bonanza.

9. Get on the national board of directors. For all of the obvious reasons previously stated, this is desirable.

10. Become a mentor. Mentoring is a great way to give back to your professional association. The often surprising bonus of mentoring is that you can learn a lot from young people entering your profession. Mentoring is also a great way to renew your network and extend your reach.

Special Events and Sponsorships

Think global, work local: Local events offer great promotional opportunities for small businesses at a relatively low cost. If you opened a café and you just found out through the chamber of commerce that the town will be sponsoring a two-week antiques fair, check with the event organizers about the cost of operating a booth at the fair. You might make money from food sales as well as have the opportunity to put your business in front of hundreds of potential customers. A masseuse might set up a table outside a local convention center and offer massages to the weary participants. If there isn't an opportunity to have a booth or hand out information about your business at a special event, look into sponsorships. If there is a music series being offered through the local children's museum and you have a kids' clothing store, look into the costs of helping out as a sponsor. For a low cost you could have an ad in the music program guide and your logo on flyers and banners.

Social Networking

LinkedIn and Facebook and Twitter, oh my. Every business in the world is working to find the magic in the bottle of social networking—and viral marketing in general, really— because when it works (remember how many millions of people viewed Susan Boyle's musical performance on YouTube?), the return on investment (ROI) is higher than any marketing initiative you could undertake. The challenge is that no one has figured out how to systematically make it work—which is why it is so compelling. Is a viral campaign really an organic phenomenon? The thought that it could still be possible to generate sales and enthusiasm for something without focus groups and throwing lots of resources at it is as exciting to marketers as finding the Holy Grail is to archaeologists. So for your search for the Holy Grail, we offer these tips from the social networking trenches:

1. Tweet or post regularly, but not annoyingly so. Does anyone care about the tuna fish sandwich that you had for lunch? No, but they do care if you read something that sparked interest, or are visiting a great

place. Did something funny happen? Something great? Something awful? These are the kinds of posts that spark comments and get retweeted.

2. Post photos or twitpix. Pictures are still worth more than a thousand words.

3. Follow those who follow you on Twitter.

4. Direct your Facebook and Twitter so you have to only update one, and it automatically updates the other.

5. Don't friend strangers on Facebook. That's what LinkedIn is for.

Celia Sack, Partner
Noe Valley Pet Company

Cecila Sack and her partner, Paula Harris, co-own Noe Valley Pet Company. At first Noe Valley Pet Company was a dog-walking service, but within the next two years, the women added a retail component to their business. We spoke with Celia about her experiences as a business owner and how she markets her company.

How did you launch your business?
Since we were already running the dog-walking service (word of mouth fills this business up very fast), we sent postcards about our store opening to all our clients, as well as to friends and acquaintances with pets. We also put banners in the windows of the shop announcing the opening day ("Treats for All!"), and we got a local dog-treat maker to bake us a bone-shaped cake. We sliced it up and gave it to all the dogs and had wine for the dog owners. That day we made $1,800, a figure we wouldn't hit again for six months!

Who are your customers?

Our customers are our neighbors; Noe Valley is a pretty afflu-ent neighborhood, so people are willing to spend money on their pets. We offer free delivery to our dog-walking clients, but even so, after tallying the weekend receipts, we notice a lot of our dog-walking clients shop with us. They seem to want to be loyal to us because we love their dogs and have developed ongoing relationships with them—another reason to have a ser-vice as part of your business. Weekends also tend to bring in people from across town, who are reached by advertising in a citywide magazine called *San Francisco*.

Do you use a public relations company?

No, but we do have a graphic designer who incorporates our logo and overall look into our ads, our free postcard and mag-net we give to customers, and our business cards and signage.

Tell us about your choices for the look of your advertisements.

I collect turn-of-the-century photos of people with their pets, and we use those in our ads to great effect. Since the photos are black-and-white, we save money on advertising, since color ads are more expensive.

What are your thoughts about advertising?

Many dot-coms failed because they threw all their money at advertising too early, when nobody recognized their logos, names, or even understood what they did. Advertising often works to remind people about you, not to introduce them to you. So many people come into our shop and say, "I always drive by and mean to come in, and then I saw your ad and decided to stop by."

If an ad is classy, it reinforces a current customer's confidence

and pride in shopping with you ("Hey, that's my pet store!").
With that philosophy in mind, I started advertising locally in a
neighborhood newspaper, *Noe Valley Voice*, and sponsored
any animal-related events around the city that would put the
store's logo on posters and programs such as animal shelter
galas and PAWS fun runs, which we still do. That way I saved
precious money I needed early on to get the store going, rather
than using it on big ads. After about a year, we decided to do
the *San Francisco* magazine ads, which come out once a month
and reach a larger, affluent swath of the city.

**Was there a particular advertising or marketing decision
that contributed to the growth of your business?**
Unbeknownst to us, the smartest thing we did was a sponsorship of the Gay and Lesbian Film Festival. During the festival,
our logo was up on the screen before every screening. And we
ran an ad in the festival program guide, which featured the
same photo we use on our postcard. The ad, a photo of all the
dogs in the back of our truck, had a tagline that stated that Noe
Valley Pet Company was "a mom and mom store." We couldn't
believe the response! Seems gay people like to shop at gay-
owned stores with a fanaticism we couldn't have guessed, so
we continue to do that every year. We also change our ads a
lot—not the general format, but I substitute different photos and
captions to keep people interested. You can see some of the
photos and our logo at our web site, *www.noevalleypet.com*.

**What have you learned about yourself and your business
since the launch?**
Sometimes I miss the intellectual challenges of my previous jobs.
I was a rare-book specialist at an auction house, and before that
I worked at Christie's in New York City specializing in nineteenth-
century European paintings. Pet supplies isn't rocket science, but

I love being my own boss. Combining the working part of my day with customers and dogs works beautifully!

What have you learned?
I've discovered that I am very social and enjoy interacting with people, but I've also learned to accept that I can't please all of the people all of the time. Not everyone will like me, and that's okay. I love playing with dogs at the beach, running around with them like the Pied Piper, eight wagging tails following my lead from truck to beach to truck. It's a great feeling when we all go home panting and smiling.

6

Being a Boss Sucks
But It Is Essential, and Often Satisfying

Most of us know what it's like to be an employee, but not all of us have experienced the challenges of being a boss, a role that is part parent, part teammate, part cheerleader, part teacher, and part cop. It is truly one of the most difficult things to do well. Think of all of those bosses whom you hated. But it is also one of the best opportunities in the world of business to get to know yourself better. Your employees will bring out the Glinda the Good Witch as well as the Wicked Witch of the West in you, forcing you to see yourself and your business as other people do, warts and all.

Whether you have one or twenty employees, being the boss forces you to set more policies than you knew existed, from how you want the phones answered to the number of personal days allowed. An employee—because she is another human being in *your* space—will help define your corporate culture even if you didn't know you had one. Whether you run a store or an advertising agency, your company will have a style all its own; if you hire a winner, she adds something. If she's a loser, she takes something away.

Last, hiring an employee forces you to make peace with the fact that you are now an adult, sometimes the bad gal, sometimes the heroine, but always the girl running the show. And there is no greater feeling than being that girl. Remember: If you choose to avoid being a boss by staying a one-girl band—even if you work twenty-four hours a day, seven days a week—you are putting a cap on the amount of money you can make and how much your business can grow.

Me, Myself, and I: The Pros and Cons of Staying a One-Woman Operation

Pros

You are only responsible for yourself.

You don't have to hire and fire employees.

You have to only earn enough to cover your personal and business expenses.

Your overhead is low.

Cons

The amount of work you can take on is limited.

It's easy to procrastinate if you're only worrying about yourself.

When a big client or new project comes along, you may not have enough resources to pursue the lead.

You may not be taken seriously by some people.

You will spend much of your day doing the grunt work.

What to Ask Yourself Before Interviewing

Can I afford an employee?
Employees are expensive. In addition to paying salaries, there are payroll taxes to pay and benefits you offer. Discuss your staffing needs with your accountant, and together review your projected income to see if you can afford to hire someone.

What is this employee going to do for the company?
We are talking about the specific, day-to-day duties of the employee. Make a list of them, including what you expect her to do on a daily, weekly, monthly, and annual basis. Is the work enough to fill at least forty hours per week, every week, all year long? If not, you might be able to get by with a temp, part-timer, or freelancer. While they will have far less invested in the growth of your business, these people can get the job done, often for less money and no benefits. Using temps or freelancers also lets you try out the idea of a new employee without committing to a weekly salary before you're sure you can handle it. It's a terrible thing to hire someone away from another job and then have to let them go because you were "off" in your planning.

What are the job requirements?
Now create a document that delineates your expectations and the education, experience, and skills required to accomplish the job. When we hired our first—briefly employed—assistant at YC, we created a memo that included a list of daily tasks, weekly tasks, and monthly tasks such as reading the newspapers looking for clips and story ideas, tallying the expenses to bill back to the clients, and assembling press kits.

How much should I pay?
Based on the list of responsibilities and requirements you have outlined, determine what you think the level of the position is. Do you need a secretary, assistant, manager, or vice president? Once you have the title, it is time to start researching the salary range for this position. To find out current salaries, Carol DuBose, owner of WorkLife Strategies, recommends "reading articles published through the Society for Human Resource Management and talking to colleagues in similar industries."

Finding Candidates

Your Social and Professional Circle
This is often the best place to start looking for an employee. Tell everyone you know that you are looking for someone and share the top-line

job requirements. Remember to thank whoever helps you to fill the position. Ti Martin, of the family-owned Commander's Palace restaurant in New Orleans, tells us that they are "superfortunate that most of our employees come to us by reputation or a friend will call and say, 'You should talk to this person.'" Sending the job post to your network on LinkedIn and Facebook is another free avenue.

Employment Agency

Employment agencies will charge you a fee (usually a percentage of the new employee's annual salary), but they and their networks can save you a great deal of time by prescreening applicants. Think of them as your "temp" Human Resources Department. If you are looking for someone in a more senior role, such as a manager or vice president, choose an executive search firm.

| the word | **Jamie Pennington, Founder**
Flexible Executives |

Jamie Pennington started her business, Flexible Executives (www.flexibleexecutives.com), to help her clients find fully vetted executives who are available for project work rather than full-time positions. Because more companies are turning to cost-saving measures like hiring a high-level executive for a short-term project only, we thought she would be the perfect person to talk to about hiring a search firm.

How do executive search firms work?
Typically executive search firms are hired by employers on a retainer or commission basis to fill senior level positions within the company.

Can you offer a few interview tips for us?
When using a search firm, much of the initial criteria has already been vetted by the search firm, so you can use your

interview to really get specific with the candidate. Ask detailed and pointed questions about their experience in relation to your company, and do not be afraid to throw curveballs to see how the candidate reacts. Additionally, you should ask open-ended questions and let the candidate speak until completion, i.e., "What can you bring to this position?" Create one or two scenario situations and pose them to the candidate to see how they would react.

How can a business owner best work and communicate with a search firm?

Many search firms work only with clients of a certain size, so the Internet continues to be a good resource, but be sure you obtain references as well. As great as the Internet can be, word of mouth and personal experience remain the best kinds of referrals!

What can a business owner expect from their search firm?

When hiring a search firm, clients are assigned a relationship manager who will interview them and their team to get a detailed assessment of their needs. Usually within a week, the business owner will be presented with various candidates who could be a good fit, and will start reviewing résumés. Once the résumés are reviewed, candidates are selected to interview, a process that varies by business owner. Some clients want only to interview a candidate once or twice, but a majority have telephone interviews, followed by in-person interviews and visits to the company office. The search firm can help negotiate salary once the ideal candidate is identified, and then the candidate is offered the position.

What are the advantages and disadvantages to using a search firm?

One of the best advantages is it saves the business owner a significant amount of time. Finding the right people can be a huge distraction from your core business. The other advantage is bringing people in from outside your usual circles. Sometimes it makes more sense to hire someone from a different industry, background, etc., to offer new contacts. Using people outside of your circle can widen your net and often bring a different perspective. The disadvantage is cost, because a traditional search firm hiring a full-time employee is usually paid a percentage of the salary. That's one of the reasons we started Flexible Executives, because we offer great people on a project-price basis, which allows business owners to expand and contract on an as-needed basis.

Trade Publications/Web Sites

Many industry magazines and web sites feature classified ads, and most professional associations distribute newsletters that list job openings.

On-line

If you decide to list the position with an on-line service, chances are good that it will be inundated with hundreds of résumés. The downside is that you might spend hours deleting e-mails, but the upside is that this approach offers you an inexpensive snapshot of the marketplace: who's looking for jobs and the salary they expect.

Local Newspapers

The most traditional method of hiring can still be a cost-effective way of filling a position. We recommend listing only a general e-mail or fax—no personal or company names. You don't want potential applicants interrupting your workday. Find out from your local paper what day the Sunday ad section closes—that's by far the best day to run help-wanted ads, and you don't want to miss the deadline.

WHAT IS YOUR FAVORITE TV SHOW?
(AND OTHER INTERVIEW QUESTIONS THAT WILL
TELL YOU ABOUT A POTENTIAL EMPLOYEE)

What are your favorite magazines?

If you run a food-related PR firm like we do, and the person answers *Scientific American*, she is probably not the right person for the job. But if she answers *Food & Wine*, then perhaps she is—unless she's just a savvy interviewee who did her homework. Hey, that's not a bad sign either.

If I called your most recent former employer and asked her what she thought your greatest weakness was, what would she say?

Sounds harsh, but think about it. Candidates have to answer this one honestly because you might call that employer for a reference. If they respond with something generic and vague like, "I work too hard," then press them on it until you get something more telling. Everyone has strengths and weaknesses, and you want employees who are aware of the areas in which they could improve and will strive to do so.

If I called your former employer and asked her what she thought your greatest strength was, what do you think she would say?

This is a gift. An opportunity for your candidate to sell herself. If she wows you, that's a good sign. If she responds with a blank stare or claims she can't select from among her innumerable wonderful traits, move along.

What was your favorite course in college and why?

This is a great question for younger candidates, and you will be surprised by the variety of responses. We've heard everything from "journalism" (good answer for our business) to "I was more into the social life" (bad answer, even though it's probably true for many of us).

How do you organize projects and responsibilities?

This is a much better question than "Do you consider yourself an organized person?" If they are really organized, they will have a system to keep track of what they need to do each day (Outlook; to-do list; the old, reliable desk calendar).

How much do you know about my business?

This question assumes that when you called or e-mailed to schedule the interview, you divulged the company information we suggested you withhold in your job postings. If the candidate doesn't know anything about what you do, that is a bad sign. If she doesn't know specifically what your company does but does know a lot about the field, that's not so bad. If she's researched you on the Internet prior to your interview and actually has good questions about you and your history, that's a great sign of initiative and resourcefulness.

What was your favorite job and why?

This is another good one for getting her to share how she works. If her favorite job was working at an answering service and she liked it because the phones were always ringing off the hook and she took pride in making sure that the doctor got to the hospital in the middle of the night to deliver a baby, then it shows she likes a fast pace and takes pride in her work. However, if her favorite job was the summer job she had as a lifeguard because she could sit in the sun all day, watch out!

Reminder: Check references, and be diligent at cross-examination. One reference check can usually lead to a network of others that taken together should give you an accurate picture of your candidate.

Stay Away! (Who Not to Hire and Why)

We need to get the legalities out of the way: You cannot base your hiring decision on anything other than the ability of the candidate. Does she have the skills to get the job done? Period. You cannot discriminate based on race, sex, religion, or sexual preference (check with your attorney about federal employment-practices laws, and go to the Equal Employment Opportunity Commission's web site at *www.eeoc.gov*). And you shouldn't anyway; it's bad karma. But what you should do is listen during an interview. Do you get a good vibe? Does she have relevant experience? Enthusiasm for the position? How does she talk about former employers? (This could be you one day.) Is she soft-spoken? (Not great for sales or public relations.) Is she aggressive? (Might be perfect for a collections agency.) Is this someone you can spend eight to ten hours a day with, five days a week? Carol DuBose doesn't hire candidates who "fail to project energy or passion for their work, or who present a victimlike attitude." This stuff is important. Ti Martin says, "I won't hire people who say, 'I'm a people person'—so cliché, even if it is true." If you are a one-woman band, you are doubling the size of your company, and a new employee will have a big impact on your professional life.

Do not hire a friend
This can be a minefield. If your new friend-employee doesn't respect that this is your company, or is just doing a poor job, it will be really awkward when you have to confront her. Also if you have several employees, hiring a friend will put her in an uncomfortable position with colleagues who might suspect favoritism.

Do not hire a neighbor
If things work out, great. Except that every time you see her on the street, you will think of work. If things don't work out, every time you see her on the stairs, you will think of firing her.

Do not hire an ex

The chances that you two are still friendly enough for you to consider hiring your ex are slim, but if you are . . . put it out of your mind! How would you feel if that person started dating your assistant? *Grrr.*

Do not hire a former boss or even a former assistant

These relationships carry professional baggage. The former boss might see you as an eternal underling, and your former assistant might constantly be fighting for recognition as something other than an assistant. Yes, there are exceptions to every rule, but this is the rule.

Do not hire a friend of one of your employees

That's right—they will chitchat, take lunch together, laugh, have a gay ol' time. And they'll while away the workday while alienating other employees.

TEN TIPS FOR TAKING YOURSELF SERIOUSLY, SO YOUR EMPLOYEE DOES TOO

1. Be on time every day
It's your business. Lead by example.

2. Don't make a habit of leaving early
Your employees will resent you if you walk out the door at three and call them from the gym at five thirty to check in.

3. Don't go drinking with your assistant
Or swap stories. Again, you're the adult now. You need to set the example. What you do in your private time away from the office should remain fodder for your peers, not your subordinates. Even when you're dying to tell someone about last night's disastrous date, resist the urge.

4. Don't ask them to do anything that is not work-related

It's rude and fosters resentment. This includes walking your dog, picking up your dry cleaning, and buying your personal holiday presents, unless, of course, the job is personal assistant.

5. Don't let them hear you on personal calls

Again, you are the adult. Not only will they imitate you for months if they hear you refer to your husband as "Dr. Love," they will feel entitled to be on their own calls all day.

6. You are not their friend

Be a pleasant boss, but never leave the door open to talk about the dating drama. You will want your employee to feel comfortable talking to you about serious personal problems (especially if they will impact her job performance); a sick mother or child-care problem, for example. But the last thing you can afford is to become a surrogate therapist for employee dating or marital woes.

7. Pitch in when you can

If you have assigned what you know to be a tedious task, such as mailing five hundred company brochures, spend at least a few minutes pitching in. This is your team; make it happen together. A little willingness to get your hands dirty will go a long way when you need a really big ditch dug.

8. Do not share company financial issues or problems

If your employees suspect things are not going well, they will be looking for another job before you know it. There is a whole philosophy of open-book management that works in big public companies (the law requires it, anyway), but in small companies you don't need your employees second-guessing your decisions.

9. If something goes wrong with a client or customer, you have to take the blame

As the boss, you are responsible for everything running smoothly. If you have a problem employee, you need to monitor her closely, provide more training, or let her go. You cannot make bad employees the scapegoats for mistakes.

10. Manage, but don't smother

Granted this is your business and you've got the most to lose, but you've got to let your employees take responsibility for their workload. Guide, cajole, pester—don't suffocate.

Final note

For loads more ideas, check out our book on management: *The Girl's Guide to Being a Boss (Without Being a Bitch)*.

The Manual (The Importance of Writing an Employee Manual)

There are several reasons for creating an employee manual right away, even if, for now, you're all alone. Essentially, you are an employee of your company, so the rules you set for yourself will dictate the tone and structure for anyone else who comes to work for you. Carrie Levin, of Good Enough to Eat restaurant, says that her employee manual "helps me enforce the regulations of my restaurant without having it be a personal confrontation." Second, when you do hire your first employee, it is far easier to have a document you can give her to read than it is to sit down and answer a million policy questions. The Department of Labor web site, *www.dol.gov*, provides all the regulations for businesses. Many are not relevant to small businesses; however, the DOL provides a good guideline of fair policies. You can also check out *www.hr-guide.com/data/ 023.htm* for sample employee handbooks and human resources consultants. If you are starting a bigger operation, it will be worth the investment to get some outside help.

Ask each employee to sign a letter indicating that she has received and read the manual and is responsible for knowing what your policies are and following them to the letter. This will help protect you if you need to fire someone down the road for not abiding by the rules.

Policies to Consider

The Fair Labor Standards Act of 1938

The Fair Labor Standards Act (FLSA) establishes standards for minimum wages, overtime pay, record keeping, and child labor. These standards apply to businesses with employees who engage in interstate commerce. The act does not cover enterprises doing less than $500,000 in business a year. There are many exempt workers, including students, service workers, and fishermen, to name just a few. If you are opening a restaurant or retail business where you will have a large number of employees, you should review the laws closely at *www.dol.gov/asp/programs/guide.htm*.

Office Hours

Set reasonable work hours as well as lunch and other breaks. Make sure your employees understand that the schedule isn't flexible without advance permission. Also have a system for rewarding those who put in extra hours to get the job done, with either comp time or bonus pay.

Payday

Determine how often you will pay people, and let them know when they should expect a check.

Vacation Time

Set a fair and reasonable vacation policy, such as two paid weeks a year. We suggest giving employees five days after each six months. Avoid having an employee ask for a two-week vacation after she's only spent three months on the job. Also consider setting a "use it or lose it" policy—if employees don't use their vacation time each year, it expires. This will keep workaholics from taking an eight-week vacation after four years without one.

Health, Dental, and Life Insurance

The federal and state governments have laws about what type of benefits you are required to make available. As a small business owner, you might not be required to pay for 100 percent of a benefit, but you must offer a company policy in which the employee can elect to pay for them. Consider your benefits program carefully. It is a great thing to offer, but remember, what you offer one, you must offer to all. So, if you want to grow to twenty employees in the first year, benefits will become a significant, possibly prohibitive cost.

Sick Days

According to the Department of Labor, the average paid sick leave is eight days after a year of service.

Personal Days

These are days that employees can use to get important things done without sacrificing vacation time. Examples of personal-day uses are funerals, moving, and religious holidays not recognized by the company.

Holidays

Make the list, check it twice, and stick to it. Think about how you will handle Jewish/Christian/Muslim holidays, Martin Luther King Jr. Day, and others that may or may not apply to you personally.

Jury Duty

The FLSA does not require payment for time not worked, including jury duty, which makes this policy a tough one to create. Ideally someone doing her civic duty should not be penalized, but you can't afford to pay someone if she gets put on a big case and could be out of work for a month a more. Consider offering five days paid jury time, and be sure that, at the conclusion of her duty, the employee brings you a court-certified receipt confirming the days served.

Family and Medical Leave Act

If you start a business that has fifty or more employees, you must grant an employee who has worked full-time for a year or more, up to a total of twelve workweeks of unpaid leave during any twelve-month period for one or more of the following reasons:

- for the birth and care of the newborn child of the employee

- for placement with the employee of a son or daughter for adoption or foster care

- to care for an immediate family member (spouse, child, or parent) with a serious health condition

- to take medical leave when the employee is unable to work because of a serious health condition

For any updates and additional information on FMLA, go to *www.dol.gov.*

Company Standards

Think about such subjects as ethics, dress code, harassment, use of company computers, personal telephone calls, smoking, e-mail, and business confidentiality and about how you expect people to act on the job. Put it all in writing.

Retirement Plans

One way to attract and keep good employees is by offering a "qualified retirement plan." Established under the Internal Revenue Code, if certain requirements are met, a qualified plan is exempt from taxation. Employers are able to deduct contributions made to the plan, while employees are not taxed until funds are distributed or not at all if they are over fifty-five.

When structured carefully, the right type of plan will offer the self-employed individual or the majority owner of a closely held corporation a substantial benefit. Some of the most common plans are money purchase, profit sharing, 401(k), SIMPLE IRA, and SEP plans.

Different types of plans will appeal to businesses of different structures, sizes, and number of employees. Each type of plan will have different rules. Some key rules are those regarding eligibility, vesting, participation, and limits on contributions. These rules must be followed carefully to avoid problems with the Internal Revenue Service.

The first step is to identify your needs and goals. Are there specific individuals (yourself or key employees) who you wish to reward more than others? Are you and your key employees older or younger in age? Does your business employ full-time and seasonal workers? What is the typical type of plan being offered by your competitors? Are you having trouble retaining employees?

Next identify how much you are prepared to set aside in employer benefits each year for yourself and your employees. Will you be able to make a contribution every year? Do you wish to have some ability to suspend contributions in not-so-good years? Are you committed to funding the plan every year?

Finally you must figure out the costs, in both dollars and administrative time, for establishing and maintaining a plan. Depending on the type of plan, these costs could be minimal or significant. It is important to address the complexities and fees related to different types of plans. Many payroll companies such as ADP offer counsel and administration of retirement plans as one of their services.

If you believe that a retirement plan could benefit your business, talk with your accountant. She can help you choose among the different types of plans and find the one that best suits your needs.

TYPES OF RETIREMENT PLANS

Money Purchase

Money purchase plans are great for employees but can be extremely costly for business owners, because once they create the program they have to pay in every year. Annual mandatory contributions of a specified percentage of each participating employee's compensation (up to 25 percent) is paid to an account set up for that employee—regardless of company profits. The employee's account balance at retirement depends on the employee's years of service, as with a profit-sharing plan, and your plan's investment performance. A money purchase pension plan may be used in conjunction with a profit-sharing plan. Self-employed individuals must reduce their contribution to 20 percent of "earned income," which is defined as gross earnings less business expenses (including plan contributions made on behalf of the employees but not the owner) and half of the owner's self-employment tax.

Profit Sharing

Profit-sharing plans are qualified plans where employers may make discretionary contributions, which may vary from year to year (to a maximum of 25 percent of eligible compensation and $49,000 annually). Generally, each employee receives the same contribution, unless the plan is specifically designed to take advantage of rules that allow senior management increased compensation. Contributions are usually based on business profits, but according to the IRS rules, you can also contribute to your plan based on compensation. For sole proprietorships, there are exceptions for contributions made by the employer for her own account as an employee if the business did not have a profit. Contributions are tax-deductible and earnings accumulate on a tax-deferred basis.

401(k)

A 401(k) plan is a defined contribution plan that is a cash or deferred arrangement. Your employee can elect to defer receiving a portion of her salary, which is instead contributed on her behalf, before taxes, to the 401(k) plan. You can choose to match employees' contributions or not. There are special rules governing the operation of a 401(k) plan, including a dollar limit on the amount you may elect to defer each year.

SIMPLE IRA

A small business pension plan, called SIMPLE, for Savings Incentive Match Plan for Employees, is set up for tax-deductible contributions of up to $11,500 a tax year beginning in 2009. Employers match the contribution, and the money isn't taxed until withdrawn.

SEP

SEPs are the least complicated retirement savings plans. A SEP allows employees or self-employed individuals to make contributions on a tax-favored basis (pretax dollars) to a personal individual retirement account. SEPs are subject to minimal reporting and disclosure requirements.

Small businesses can also elect to have employees defer salary into SEPs on a before-tax basis, with limits on the total amounts contributed each year.

Reimbursable Expenses

Explain what you will reimburse employees for, such as local taxis, after-hours meals, entertaining clients (with preapproval), or purchasing office supplies.

Overtime Pay

Set a policy about overtime pay for nonhourly (exempt) employees. If your employees are hourly workers, the law requires you pay them overtime. There are three classifications of exemption from the Fair Labor Standards ACT: Exempt Executive (or Managerial), Exempt Administrative, and Exempt Professional. For a complete explanation of the exemptions please visit *www.dol.gov/whd/fisa/index.htm*.

Performance Reviews

Never include in a manual a percentage for salary increases or even if you *will* give raises. But do include a schedule for reviews. You may want to think about an initial review three months after an employee's first day and then annual reviews after that.

Once you have these issues outlined in your mind, write them down. This document will become the backbone of your employee manual. You can then add pages, or adjustments, as they become necessary for you and your staff.

Building Loyalty: Keeping Those You Love

A great employee is trustworthy, represents your business well to the outside world, helps you generate (or retain) business, respects your authority, and is a positive influence on other employees. These are the people you want to keep. They are the chosen few whom you will want to pay a higher salary down the line, but trust us, if they are great, it will be worth every penny to keep them. Carol DuBose shows appreciation for her employees by offering to pay for a class or training program that her employees wish to attend to add to their skills. Ti Martin says, "Be kind, have fun, acknowledge people, and try to get them to push themselves. Try to make them be an even better person than they thought they could be."

Show them the love!

Increased Responsibility

Any good employee wants more responsibility. Giving it to her helps you both.

Comp Time

If your employee has been putting in long hours or coming in on the weekend, show your appreciation by giving her a day off. Another inexpensive way to show a little love.

Promotion

Lofty titles are free for the giver but can make or break an employee's decision to look for another job.

Management Every Day

The day-to-day management of employees is something that you can improve on a daily basis. Great managers are rare. Despised ones are all too common. Don't expect yourself to be perfect from the beginning. Shooting for "fair" is a good initial target. Just remember the golden rule: Manage as you would like to be managed. Be fair, be respectful, be clear, set rules, and stick to them across the board. Easy to say. Hard to do. Here are some tips:

the word	**Carrie Levin, Chef/Owner** Good Enough to Eat

Carrie Levin has operated Manhattan's Good Enough to Eat restaurant for more than two decades. She has faced many staff changes in that time period and here shares some tips she has learned along the way.

_____

I try to keep regular schedules for my staff. It is something they can depend on, and it adds structure to what can be a very chaotic business.

If my employees need to leave early for personal reasons, that is fine with me. They know that I understand and respect that they have a life outside of my restaurant, and in return, if I need them to stay late, they do.

If my staff has a problem with me or with how we run the business, they write it up anonymously on one of our customer-comment cards because they know I respond to every single one.

Meetings, Meetings, and Not Too Many Meetings

At one of our previous jobs, management instituted a policy of weekly meetings. _Everybody_ had weekly meetings. You had a "weekly" with your direct supervisor. They had a "weekly" with their direct supervisor, and so it went, right up the chain of command to the corner office. In addition to our personal "weekly," each department had a "weekly." By the end of the week, you hadn't gotten any work done because you (or someone you needed) were always tied up in a "weekly." Don't go overboard with meetings.

But it is important to set some meetings and routines for reporting in your company. Some managers have a daily "homeroom" that serves two purposes: (1) it gets everyone on the same page, and (2) it gets everyone to work on time. For others, weekly meetings are enough. This is a place to introduce new policies and new employees and make general announcements. Smaller groups can review or set deadlines, give feedback, and assign new projects. Choose a meeting day and time, and stick to it. It helps everyone plan the rest of their schedule.

Your Door Stays Open
This does not mean that you are there to listen to their complaints. Rather, let everyone know that you are always available for professional help or advice.

Check In, but Don't Smother
You need to keep tabs on everything without being oppressive—a tightrope act if ever there was one. Set step deadlines along the way to any big project. If you find that they are not being met or employees are running into problems, you need to be a bit more involved. If things are going smoothly and they are getting it done right the first time, then lucky you! Praise the hell out of these talented employees and then focus your energies elsewhere.

Constructive Feedback
All the management books try to tell you how to give employees constructive feedback. "Start out by saying things like, 'This is in the right direction, but this paragraph needs some work,' or 'You were a little tentative in that meeting, maybe next time we should rehearse together.'" Based on our own experience, we strongly urge you to head off problems before they blow up in your face. If an employee is going to make a presentation in a client meeting, make her rehearse for you first. If she stinks, you present and let her try again the next time. This isn't the school play; it's business. It's not about egos; it's about getting the job done right. If she is sending out external correspondence, edit and proofread it first, and be honest and thorough in your revisions. Help

your good employees learn from their mistakes, and be open to giving them opportunities the next time around.

Nip It in the Bud

We once had an assistant who, from the first day of her employment, spelled names wrong on phone messages. If a person called multiple times, each time the name was recorded differently. This was irritating and confusing. We tried to be kind. When she handed us a message, we would say, "Oh, this must be Joe Smith, not Jo Smython." We figured she would get the message and simply start asking people how to spell their names. Didn't happen. And on the fifteenth day of her employ, after the umpteenth mangled name, we yelled at her—unnecessary and avoidable bad-boss behavior, which could have been headed off if we had simply told her on day one or two how important it is for us to get clear phone messages. Moral of the story: Be clear and direct about what you need.

There's No "I" in "TEAM"

If you are running a small business, establish yourself as a member of the project team and have accountability to other members. Carrie Levin tells us that her employees always know that she is available to jump in when things get busy. "Whenever it gets crazy at the restaurant, I do anything I can to help out, bussing tables, refilling coffee, taking orders, whatever needs to happen."

Share Your Calendar

If your business forces you to be away from the office most of the day in meetings, it's a good practice to post your calendar so that your employees know what you're up to and can find you if they need you.

Don't Be a Snob

Be seen at the copier, fax machine, and in the mailroom. Ti Martin says that she tries to "walk the talk of team." When it is your business, you are not above doing anything. Also there's no more subtle way of communicating that you expect everyone to know how to operate the copier, fax, and postage machine than by having them see you strut your stuff on that equipment. But be reasonable. If you are on deadline for a client, don't get bogged down by pitching in on the grunt work.

Get People Excited about Every Project

When assigning a task or a project, show enthusiasm for it. Encourage your employees to take ownership of the task or project by making them feel special. Try out a lead-in like, "You would be great for this," or, "We had you in mind when we decided to take this on."

Get Things Done ASAP

It is important to set an example, so get things done as quickly as you want them done. If someone gives you something to sign, approve, or edit—do it right away.

Throwing the Rest Back: Firing with Dignity
(The First Time Is the Hardest)

Firing someone is never easy. You are going to become a negative part of her employment history. You will forever be known as "the jerk who fired me." Knowing that, and knowing that you are cutting off someone's income flow (at least until some other sucker hires her), makes it difficult to fire *well*. In fact, we are not yet convinced that you can fire *well*. But you can, at the least, fire with *dignity* (we are talking about your own here). And boy, have we lost some along the way.

How Not to Do It (Dignity-Losing "Non-firings")

Women don't like to be bad gals. We want everybody to like us. But by trying to be the nice girl, we can undermine our authority as employers and lose some dignity in the process. From the countless women we have spoken to about this, we have heard the same thing: The first time it was awful; after that, it was a breeze.

SCENARIO #1: We once had an assistant who wasn't working out. We hired her on a probationary basis (that is, with the understanding that we would evaluate whether to keep her after a defined period of time) and wanted to sack her before the time was up. But she was young, and we are nice people, so we wanted to soften the blow. Here's what we said: "We're really sorry. We really like you, but we just can't afford you right now. We are going to have to let you go. We feel terrible. We hope you can understand."

Employee 1, Employer 0

This is *not* firing someone. This is a layoff and not a very good one. And of course, laid-off employees don't "understand." You are rejecting them and taking away their financial security. They will never feel sympathy for you and the problems that the company may or may not have. These are not their problems. But at the end of the day, their livelihood and happiness are not *your* problems. Would you expect your customers to pay you for a bad job or a job not done at all? Of course not. Well, you are basically your employees' customer. If they don't deliver, you shouldn't pay. Emotionally, this may be complicated. But professionally, it's as simple as that.

Again, it's about self-respect, sitting at the grown-ups' table, and treating yourself and your business with dignity. Couching a termination in the humane language of a "layoff" is a cop-out and could have serious repercussions. Most likely, the employee will share her news (and spin what you told her) with other employees, creating a negative ripple effect throughout the business.

SCENARIO #2: We hired a freelancer with the option to join the staff after a three-month probationary period. At the end of the three months, we felt that she wasn't the right person for the job. But again, we didn't want to hurt her feelings. We wanted to make her feel that she was making the choice to leave. Here's what we said: "We like you, but, well, we don't think this is working out. Do you? We don't think this is right for us. Do you?"

Employee 2, Employer 0

Again, this is *not* terminating an employee. This is begging her to take the blood off your hands. You know what, Lady Macbeth? Take the blood. You've earned it. Your hard work and energy has made the company, and if this person's energy is draining the company, she has got to go. As painful as it is, if employees have no contract, you have every right to terminate their employment. Feel bad about it? Sure. Have a martini and a cigarette after work to drown your sorrows? Okay, just this once. Work out your tension in a kickboxing class at the gym? Great idea. Just be sure you do what needs to be done to protect your interests.

The Right Way (A Dignified-Yet-Compassionate Firing)
"Unfortunately this isn't working out. We've pointed out areas where we needed you to improve a few weeks back, but you haven't corrected them. We are going to have to ask you to leave. Please pack up your desk (or locker), and one of us will show you out."

How you kept your dignity: Scary, right? Well, this method does many things for you. It is a clean break that leaves no room for negotiation. You do not want the ex-employee talking to your staff on the way out about how awful you are. You are not giving her the opportunity to take any important documents, disks, or files with her. It's for the best. If it'll make you feel better, offer her two weeks pay as severance, but don't ask her to stay for those two weeks—chances are she'll just spread her discontent.

Things to Remember When Firing Someone

- If an employee is not right for you, chances are you are not right for her.

- Take a spiritual approach. Maybe she is meant to be doing something else with her life and you are just pushing her in the right direction.

- If she has been unhappy working for you, she is probably poisoning the minds of others in your company. You and your other employees are better off with her gone.

- Don't take her anger personally. It's business. Let it (and her) go.

- It is not your entire responsibility to make someone a good employee. If you have given clear directions and feedback and she still isn't coming through, it's on her. Not you. Most important (this should be your mantra from this day on), this is YOUR COMPANY. You make the decisions and take the risks. If someone isn't right for you, then she has to leave.

TEN TIPS FOR HOW TO ASSIST YOURSELF (IF YOU CAN'T AFFORD AN ASSISTANT)

1. The to-do list is your friend
As the last thing you do before you finish work for the day, take a moment to go over your to-do list and update it for the next day. The successful Franklin Planner folks recommend you take fifteen minutes of quiet time a day to organize your to-do list.

2. Spend one hour a day on office duties
Don't let the pile of filing, faxing, and mailing get out of control—especially the billing. It's very easy to be too tired to sit down and write up an invoice if you are a personal trainer or massage therapist who spends all day running around to see clients. Make the time. You may not need more than an hour a week.

3. Have the right attitude
Running your own business is stressful. Use downtime to relax.

4. Be smart about e-mail
Instead of sitting there watching and waiting for e-mails (unless that is your entire job), check them a few times throughout the day. Once

when you get in, after lunch, and before you leave might work. Responding right away will minimize work spilling over into the next day.

5. Spend minimal time on personal e-mail
Don't spend hours sifting through spam mail, forwarded jokes, and the occasional work-related e-mail.

6. File right the first time
Save yourself future headaches by creating a filing system that makes sense right away and later.

7. Do it today
Don't put off errands like bank deposits and trips to the post office. The pile will only grow and grow.

8. Know your office supplies
Read the catalogs that arrive addressed to Office Manager, because that is now you. Order right, order smart, and don't overorder office supplies.

9. Stock up on mailing supplies
There are almost always long lines at the post office. If you run out of stamps, envelopes, or boxes in the middle of the day, you don't want to waste precious business hours in line. So plan ahead and stock up. Or, order everything on-line and have supplies delivered to you.

10. Sign up for service
Set up accounts with UPS, Federal Express, DHL, a local messenger service, a temp agency, and any other service that you can call for pickups, deliveries, or helping hands. You do not have time to deliver packages.

Keeping It Legal

You will need to speak with your lawyer and accountant about the details of hiring an employee, because many of the laws change from year to year. You can also check with the Department of Labor for answers to basic questions at *www.dol.gov*. We wouldn't be helpful fellow-girls if we didn't give you a few questions to ask your lawyer and accountant.

Questions for Your Lawyer

- What are the details of the Americans with Disabilities Act (ADA)?
- What are the Equal Employment Opportunity Commission (EEOC) guidelines?
- What are the federal and state laws regarding questions I can't ask a job applicant?
- What are the requirements of the Family and Medical Leave Act (FMLA)?
- What are the state and federal laws about firing an employee?
- What is COBRA?
- What are the laws governing health-care policies for small businesses?
- What are the guidelines of the Fair Labor Standards Act (FLSA)?
- What are the guidelines of the Occupational Safety and Health Administration (OSHA)?

Questions for Your Accountant

- Can you explain the advantages and disadvantages of the various types of retirement plans?
- How do I account for tips that my employees receive?

- Do I need to pay overtime?

- What forms do my new employees need to fill out?

- How do I pay their payroll taxes?

- Is it worth it for me to hire a payroll company, and what exactly do they do?

Susan Mussaffi
Owner, Organic Cottontail

Before launching Organic Cottontail Kingdom, Susan spent ten years at Morgan Stanley working in information technology. When she turned forty, she realized that she had many dreams that had yet to be realized, including traveling and owning her own business. Her childhood dream of becoming an entrepreneur became a reality when she launched Organic Cottontail soon after quitting her job. When figuring out how to structure her business, she decided early on that she would use freelancers and outsource her fulfillment. Thanks to her years at Morgan Stanley, she knew that she needed to focus on her core competencies so that she could grow her business. With so many small businesses taking advantage of the increasing volume of high-quality freelancers in the marketplace, we spoke to Susan about how she hires independent contractors to make her retail business work.

How many independent contractors do you work with over the year and for what kinds of jobs?
I work with approximately fifteen contractors over the course of a year to help me with graphic design, web development, photography, clothing design, package design, pattern making, sample making, and I have a village of artisans who make my boxes.

Why did you decide to go the freelance route, and is there a point when you would consider hiring full-time?

I think there is a cost-time benefit to going the freelance route when you are starting your business. I knew someone who would spend several hours a day picking, packing, and mailing products. I found a fulfillment center in Missouri, MarketTech 1, which provides me with amazing pricing and customer service. But I do think there will be a point in the future where it will make sense.

How do you find your freelancers? Do you interview them? Call references?

I have found many graphic designers through Elance and Odesk. These sites give a lot of user feedback, including ratings. I have had some very bad and scary experiences with free-lancers—even if I am a believer that everything happens for a reason and a lesson must be learned. You could be giving the keys to your castle away, so you need to be careful and check references. Skype has been an amazing tool. Ensure that you have a backup of all files as you go through each milestone.

Does hiring a freelancer have any disadvantages?

I don't think you're always getting the cream of the crop. I have been fortunate because some of my freelancers were in school and had a great work ethic. I have had issues with keeping to timelines, so it's best to factor this in. In general, it has been cost-effective, because you pay as you go instead of the up-front investment with employees.

Tell us about your first firing experience of one of your contractors.

I had a contractor who destroyed all my files and took my site down. He threatened that he would tell lies about me using social media. I managed to calm things down and he apologized, but he was fired!

Do you have any hiring advice?
Yes. Keep requirements simple, ensure candidates have expertise in the area you are looking for, and negotiate a fair price.

Do you have any advice for managing freelancers?
Ensure that your needs and expectations are simple, clear, and documented. It might be a good idea to ask for status reports on your projects and remember that kindness and appreciation go a long way.

Do you have any advice for those just starting their own businesses?
Listen to the little voice in your tummy and trust your instincts, and network with women's organizations such as Collective-E for support and contacts.

7

Acting Like an Adult
Finding Your Voice and Professional Style

Have you ever looked at the most prominent women in our society, the Oprah Winfreys, Hillary Clintons, and Maria Shrivers, and wondered, "How do they exude such confidence, smarts, and power?"

If you harbor hopes of going into business, the question takes on a personal significance: "How could *I* ever exude such confidence, smarts, and power?" It's a challenge every emerging businesswoman faces. How do you go from being the student to being the teacher? From being the employee to being the boss?

In some ways, the answer is the same as the one to the age-old question, when do you go from being a child to being an adult? There is no single moment at which you get to proclaim, "I'm an adult." Maturation is a lifelong process; you're always learning and growing and getting better at being the person you want to be.

It's the same in business. You never cross that invisible finish line; you're always honing your skills, getting better at being the queen bee.

The truth is that every woman we interviewed for this book had to navigate this sea of self-discovery and still occasionally feels twinges of self-doubt, even if they've owned their own business for decades. How did they, and do they, overcome? The answer is simple: by being as informed as possible, gleaning confidence from their successes, and—when all else fails—by faking it as best they can.

Nothing can take the place of real-world experience, but think of this chapter as a primer for business adulthood. In it, we will give you a road map for getting through those first client meetings, confrontations, business trips, and presentations.

Part of being an adult is being informed. So in the pages that follow, you will also find guides to modern business etiquette, key business terms, blogs to check out, and other information that will make you more of an adult in the business world or at least allow you to fake it with confidence.

How to Look Like an Adult: Finding Your Personal Style

Betty Keepin, owner of KeepinTouch Communicatons, reminds us that "first impressions do count!" And she means the whole package, including hair, clothes, makeup, the way you walk, shake hands, speak—it all sends a message to those you do business with. Betty offers this warning, "By overlooking the importance of your image and style, you're likely to convey uncertainty and low self-esteem."

So even if you feel like a kid on the inside—and if you do, you are not alone (almost every woman we interviewed for this book occasionally felt out of place in the business world)—dress like an adult on the outside. Even if you open a yoga studio, you want to check out the latest yoga fashions to add to your wardrobe. To define this new business-owner-you, we recommend that you look around at how your competitors are presenting themselves. If you are launching a professional service business, such as career consulting, executive search agency, or accounting firm, take a trip to your local department store and talk to their personal shopper about this season's professional look, and flip through magazines that are geared toward women (not teenagers), like *O, The Oprah Magazine*, to check out the new styles. If you are opening a garden shop, you will probably not be wearing a suit to work; so you might want to look through catalogs like Smith and Hawken's rather than *InStyle* magazine, to see what they offer for outdoor apparel—or you might just need to wear your most comfortable jeans. Pick a look that you feel comfortable and confident carrying off. At this point you might want to steer away from anything too radical. Launching a business is stressful enough by itself.

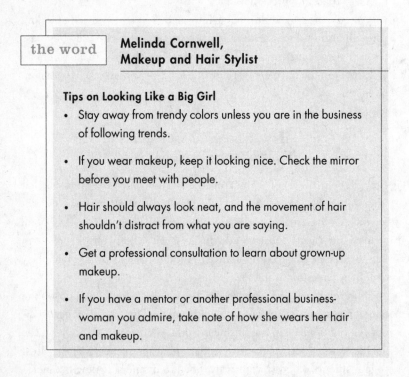

the word

**Melinda Cornwell,
Makeup and Hair Stylist**

Tips on Looking Like a Big Girl

- Stay away from trendy colors unless you are in the business of following trends.

- If you wear makeup, keep it looking nice. Check the mirror before you meet with people.

- Hair should always look neat, and the movement of hair shouldn't distract from what you are saying.

- Get a professional consultation to learn about grown-up makeup.

- If you have a mentor or another professional business-woman you admire, take note of how she wears her hair and makeup.

First New-Business Meeting—Now What?

Nothing will make you feel like a kid faster than a new-business meeting. There you are selling yourself and your business to a bunch of strangers. They might ask questions you are not able to answer; they might not laugh at your jokes; or they might cut the meeting short. Or they might not, because no two new-business meetings will be alike. After some meetings, you will feel so great about yourself and your business you will walk on air all the way back to the office. Other meetings will cause you to curl up in a ball under your desk, ruing the day you decided to do this. Since you can't control the chemistry between you and your potential client (which is often the deciding factor in whether you're hired), we suggest that you focus on what you can control. You want to leave a new-business meeting knowing that you did everything you could do to get the job.

Know Your Audience

Find out who will be at the meeting and what their role is in the company. Who is the decision maker in the group? You want to know whom you are talking to because to keep everyone engaged and sold on you, the talking points and agenda (discussion points for the meeting) should be tailored for the group. If you own a web site design business and you are meeting with an owner of a company, as well as her public relations representative, you need to make sure that in addition to offering suggestions for the design of the site, you also discuss how the design could benefit public relations activities. If you are an event planner meeting with a bride and her father, who has made it clear he will be paying for the wedding, then you want to sell them on your ideas for the budget as well as the wedding.

Know the Potential Client

Do the research: *www.google.com* is a good place to start. You want to know as much about the client as possible to help you formulate your questions for the meeting and help you answer their questions during the meeting. If you own a financial consulting business and you are meeting with a company to discuss the possibility of hiring you to help them with next year's projections, you should be completely up-to-speed about the details of their business, including size, products, market share, and potential for growth.

Know Your Company

Work out your pitch before you go to the meeting. What makes you and your business unique? And why should someone hire you over another company? Having these talking points in your back pocket will help give you confidence. If you are a freelance writer, come to the table with a client list, writing samples, and referrals. But also be ready to talk about how quick your turnaround time is.

Know Your Abilities

Practice your pitch before you meet. Have at the ready a list of things that your company does really well and examples to back it up. If you have opened a restaurant and you are meeting with a client who may buy out your restaurant for the night for a special event, then you want to mention any positive reviews you have received, the professionalism of your staff, the quality of your food, and the unique aspects of your space.

Know Your Limitations

Be realistic with yourself and the potential client about what you can and can't do. It won't do your business any good in the long run if you overpromise and end up underdelivering. You will lose respect from the business community if you get a reputation for exaggerating your abilities. However, if you want to take a stab at something that you haven't done before, then just be honest about it with clients or customers from the get-go, and charge less for the experience.

We were hired to handle the public relations campaign for Jamie Oliver's cookbook *Happy Days with the Naked Chef*. In a private meeting with Jamie, he asked us if we could go out and line up a few companies interested in sponsoring his book tour, because he wanted to create live cooking demonstrations at bookstores around the country that went above and beyond what the publisher had in mind. We had never gone after sponsors before (and having only a six-month window to set everything up made it more daunting) nor had we coordinated such an extravagant traveling road show—complete with TV screens, a drum set, 3,500 pounds of production equipment, and seven staff members—but this was a fantastic opportunity for our company to try something new and grow a little bit in the process. So we said yes and cold-called companies to get them to contribute sponsorship funds based only on our promise of a spectacular show. After securing $170,000 from sponsors—in a tough economic market—we flew in production experts from Australia and went on the road for ten days to seven cities to host eight live shows. It was a huge success, and both the sponsors and Jamie were thrilled with the attendance and the coverage of the events. Our company made only a little profit, but we gained immeasurable experience, and now we have a story that helps sell YC Media at every new-business meeting.

Ask Questions

You are interviewing them while you are being interviewed in any first meeting with a potential client or customer. So have your questions ready. These questions could range from "What are you hoping to achieve by working with us?" to "Have you worked with a company similar to ours in the past?" Also this is a great time to clarify the goals of your working relationship. This is key for our business, because often we meet with chefs who are talking to us about helping them "get more press." This is too vague for us. We need to know exactly what publications and television shows are important to their business. We also ask them how accessible they are—if we have a last-minute interview opportunity, can we find them? And most important, what are they expecting from us? If they tell us that they are hiring us to book them on *Oprah*, *Today*, and *20/20* in a single month, then this is our opportunity to set them straight.

Never Answer the Cost Question at the First Meeting

Almost every potential client or customer you will meet with will ask you during the course of your first meeting how much you charge. They will look at you expectantly, pressuring you for an answer then and there. They are hoping that you will buckle and throw out a number that you both know is low because you want to say something that will make them happy. Don't do it! Don't commit to any financial arrangement that you will regret later (minutes later). Tell them that you want some time to think about it and you will submit a proposal for them to consider. Make sure you and the potential client agree on a date for the proposal submission by the end of the meeting.

Ten Web Sites and Blogs to Follow

Knowing what is happening in the world, with your profession and in the news will help you feel like a big girl, so while you may consider *www.tmz.com* required reading, you should be hopping on-line for content that goes beyond your expertise and personal interests.

As a business owner you will do everything from advertising to organizing an office, so while you may be an expert in one area, chances are you need to learn a lot about the others. You can't delegate everything on a tight budget! Thanks to the wide range of content available on the web, learning about almost anything these days is a few clicks away. We've done some surfing on your behalf and created a list of web sites and blogs that offer a quick "101" on a variety of areas of business that you will learn about in your role as owner. Hopefully this list is in addition to the required reading you need for your business. If you are a literary agent, you should still be reading *www.publishersweekly.com*; a freelance food writer should be following *www.eater.com*; a designer should be hopping on *www.coolhunting.com*. But for business basics and insights into marketing, money, and management, check out:

Entrepreneur.com
As they describe it, this web site helps readers "start, grow, or manage a small business." It offers up-to-date tax information, management tips, franchise opportunities, business ideas, and inspiring profiles.

Workingmother.com
This site features tips on everything from how to harmonize work and life to upcoming conferences and events for working moms, and stories about moms successfully doing it all.

Time.com or Newsweek.com
If you are like many of us and don't have time to read the paper every day, spend twenty minutes on-line catching up on the state of the world, and you'll always have something to talk about with your customers.

Oprah.com

We love Oprah and we really love her web site because every day it offers articles we want to read, stories we're inspired by, recipes we want to make, and a million ideas for how to make the best of the life we've created. Most important, there is always a piece on the importance of taking time out for yourself.

Smartmoney.com

This site offers tips for investing on-line, getting savvy about personal finance, and spending wisely on things like cars, technology, and real estate. Remember we said that you will think about money all the time when you own your own business? Well, we want you to think smartly about it.

Inc.com

This great web site for small business owners is fun to read and easy to navigate. It includes timely financial guidance and tips on branding, marketing, and selling.

Huffingtonpost.com

We love this web site for its smarts, up-to-the-minute news, and wide enough platform for a range of voices and opinions on what is happening around us. The book reviews, celebrity gossip, media coverage, and blogs will make sure you remain an interesting dinner companion at your next business event.

Businessweek.com

This site may be a little dry, but it is informative, with profiles of business leaders and articles on everything from investments to the world economy. The more you read this, the more you'll talk like the businesswoman you are!

Advertisingage.com

This web site for the advertising industry offers news on all aspects of the advertising business—from campaigns that were busts to success stories. An especially helpful feature is the site's studies on marketing to specific demographics, which can help small business owners speak to their target customers.

Facebook.com, Twitter.com, and LinkedIn.com
We're including these because through social networking you can build your client base, hire a new employee, spread the news about an upcoming promotion, be introduced to potential mentors and investors, and reconnect with people from your past who could help you grow your business.

WSJ.com
The *Wall Street Journal* has a dynamic site with a section dedicated to small business. There is advice for starting an S Corporation, formulas for calculating start-up costs, and tips for building a stronger financial foundation for your business.

"I'll Have a Diet Coke"
(Drinks with Clients)

Unless we are at a conference and there are no other options, we prefer not to meet potential clients for drinks; there is just something a bit too unbusinesslike about sitting at a bar with a stranger discussing business. But if they insist, or scheduling constraints make the cocktail hour the only hour that works for both parties, then we advise that you not drink when having drinks with clients. We mean alcohol. Order mineral water, soda, or juice, and skip the booze. Why? Because it makes for a sloppy meeting. It is fine if your client wants to drink, but keep it professional and abstain. Also, if you are choosing the spot, make sure you pick a bar that has tables and is fairly quiet and private. Hotel bars are good meeting places because they are often conveniently located.

No Spaghetti and Why
(Lunch with Clients)

Meeting over lunch is not as easy as it sounds. In fact, oftentimes it is downright awkward. You may be hungry, frazzled from the commute to the restaurant, anxious about leaving your business in the middle of the day, interrupted throughout the meal by a waiter, and have difficulty squeezing in the reason for the meeting between bites. But we have some tips that will help you approach mealtime meetings with confidence.

Create an agenda before you arrive, and memorize it

While you are still at home or at the office (or at the home office), write down an agenda for the meeting. It can be very basic, something like this for a quarterly review meeting:

> Greetings
>
> Synopsis of Goals My Company Has Achieved for the Client This Quarter
>
> Synopsis of Upcoming Goals for Next Quarter
>
> Action Steps My Company Is Going to Take Next Quarter

Use the time it takes you to get to a meeting to go over the agenda, making sure to illustrate your talking points with examples, such as specific successes or, if you have them, sales or growth statistics that will show your contribution to their business.

Don't take notes while you are eating

This says to the client that you don't have the ability to remember something for longer than an hour. We recommend instead that while you are waiting for the check, you review with the client what action items were discussed over the lunch and, if necessary, as soon as you are back in your car, jot everything down.

Pick up the check

Even if they are a huge company making millions of dollars and you could not be smaller, pick up the check. Don't split it or let them wrestle it out of your hands. Ask for the check, pay the bill, and thank your client for their business. They will appreciate it.

<table>
<tr><td>the word</td><td>Betty Keepin
KeepinTouch Communications</td></tr>
</table>

Tips for Acting Like a Big Girl

- When meeting with a client over a meal, select a restaurant that makes table talk easy and is convenient for the client, preferably one you are familiar with.

- Always have a reservation and arrive early; don't keep your client waiting.

On the Road: Business Travel

The first few trips you take as an entrepreneur can be scary. To start, unless you have a partner, you are probably traveling alone. Checking into a hotel, just you and your little suitcase, can be lonely and disorienting. Arriving in a strange city for a new-business meeting can be intimidating. We believe that if you are well prepared, business travel can be fun and empowering. Let's face it, you are getting away from the office, family obligations, and bills, even if only for a day. If you take advantage of whatever downtime you have, you can use business travel as a minivacation just for you. We have had some great business trips to Chicago, San Francisco, and Los Angeles that were both productive for us and our clients as well as fun. We have also had some trips that were all work, all the time.

Where are you going?

Before you leave for a business trip, take some time to learn about the city or town where you are going. Go on-line, read a travel book, or ask your friends for restaurant and other recommendations. Even if you are going to the tiniest town in America, chances are there are some beautiful places to visit.

Get sleep

Not the easiest thing to do when you are on the road but the most important. If you are tense after a day of travel, take a bath before you go to bed or work out in the hotel's gym.

Eat breakfast

Sitting in a business meeting with your stomach grumbling can be distracting for the group and embarrassing for you. Make sure you eat breakfast, even if it means getting up a little earlier.

Read the local paper

Read the local paper every morning to give you something to talk about with whomever you meet with that day. The local paper will also offer events and local happenings that you might just have time for.

Eat well

We have a rule when it comes to business travel: We must eat well. Even if we sit through back-to-back meetings, when it comes to dinner, we check the web and ask the hotel concierge or our client where the best, not the most expensive, restaurants are. When we were on the road with one top chef, he insisted that we seek out the best steak in Houston, pulled-pork in Georgia, and gumbo in New Orleans.

Keep receipts

When traveling for business, everything you spend money on can either be billed back to a client or be used for tax deductions, so save every receipt. Carry a small expanding file folder (check-size is fine) with you and file your receipts into categories (by client or by tax category) on a daily basis. When you return to your office, you won't have a pile of receipts to wade through.

Packing lightly and rightly

The best tip we can give you for packing for a business trip is . . . pack lightly. It's no fun in these days of intense airport security to drag around huge overstuffed suitcases when you are wearing a freshly dry-cleaned suit and high heels. So pack lightly, buy yourself a suitcase with wheels, and fight for that overhead space. And remember, before you begin packing, you want to check on the weather situation. You can either call the hotel or log on to *weather.com*. This should dictate your attire and will help you fit in a bit more with whomever you are meeting.

Call ahead
Confirm your reservation with the hotel before you arrive. Get it in writing. And while you have them on the phone, see if they have irons and ironing boards and hair dryers in the rooms or can supply them. If they don't offer either, be sure you pack an iron and a hair dryer. You don't want to have wet hair and a wrinkled suit for an out-of-town business meeting.

Be your own pharmacy
Nothing is worse than feeling ill, alone in a hotel room, in the middle of a strange city. The last thing you want to do is get up and try to find a twenty-four-hour pharmacy. If you are going on the road for your business, pack your medicine cabinet. Make sure you include aspirin, tampons, antacid, sleep aids, mouthwash, toothbrush, toothpaste, dental floss, makeup, hairbrush, deodorant, and hair spray or gel. If you travel a lot, keep a kit at the ready so that you don't have to deal with this every time.

Have comfortable clothes for your downtime
By its nature, traveling is stressful, especially when you are on a business trip. So you need to take advantage of your private time. If putting on those comfortable sweats (the pair that your husband thinks are the ugliest, least-sexy thing you own) makes you feel good, throw them in the suitcase. Also remember to pack socks. Some of us, even in the summer, freeze in hotel rooms.

Pack a mini-office
Pack your laptop, cell phone and charger, BlackBerry, extra pens, calculator, notebooks, Post-it notes, and anything else that you use throughout the day at your office. You may find yourself working at night in the hotel room, checking your messages throughout the day, or organizing

yourself on the flight, so take along a mini-office. Make sure you pack this mini-office in a bag small enough to take on the plane and fit under your seat so that you can access your work during the flight. Pack extra batteries for all of your electronics and your phone charger.

Bring your own alarm

We know the hotel offers wake-up calls, but not everyone wakes up as soon as they hear a friendly voice telling them to. You are better off bringing an alarm from home with you on the road. You don't want to risk oversleeping. Knowing your alarm from home is there will let you fall asleep without anxiety about depending on the kindness of strangers to wake you.

Dress for business travel success

It isn't a bad idea to ask around to see how formal or informal the business community is where you will be visiting. We once went to a business meeting at *Amazon.com*, located in Seattle, and looked downright silly in our beige Banana Republic suits surrounded by everyone dressed in flannel shirts and sandals with socks. We also mistakenly dressed in our hip, downtown New York City outfits for a meeting with a potential client in Maryland, with dire results. We can't even count the number of times we heard, "You girls must be from New York." When people say, "You must be from . . ." that is never a good sign. Don't overhaul your personal style for a trip out of town, but do make some effort to fit in.

Giving a Presentation to Get Business: Is the Mike On?

Many of us are terrified of public speaking. If you are one of those people who would rather move to another state than talk in front of a group, it is really in your best interest as a new entrepreneur to overcome this fear. As a business owner, you want to look for opportunities to put yourself in front of potential customers and represent your business in the best way possible. The bad news for all of you who have avoided this for most of your life is that even if you don't solicit the opportunity, you will be called on at some point to participate in a public speaking engagement such as a conference for your industry, a meeting at the local chamber of commerce, or even on career day at your child's school. The good news is that there are ways to overcome your fears.

If after reading through our tips you feel that you could use some practice, join a local chapter of Toastmasters International or sign up for a public speaking course.

Giving a presentation or a talk when you are an adult business owner is nothing like giving an oral presentation to your tenth grade English class. We promise. For one thing, the members of your adult audience want to be there. They want to listen to you. They are not hoping you make a fool of yourself so they can laugh about it in the cafeteria with their friends. You are there as an expert, and chances are, you know more about the topic than your audience.

What's my line?

Prepare, prepare, prepare. Spend a lot of time preparing what you are going to talk about and how you are going to talk about it. When you write your speech, think about what you want the audience to learn from you. And what you want them to remember. Try to come up with three key pieces of information.

When we speak to a group of potential clients, the three key pieces of information we share are a brief recap of the history of YC Media, specific coverage we have obtained for our clients, and how our media contacts, experience, and enthusiasm would benefit those potential clients in the audience.

Who is the audience?

Tailor your material to your audience. If you are speaking at a trade show, the audience's knowledge might be on a par with yours, in which case you want to focus your discussion on what you learned that year or on the state of your industry today. If you are addressing local college students who are considering going into your profession, then your speech should focus on the basics of your business—what's good and bad, what the opportunities are, and what kind of education and experience are necessary to break in—so they know what they are getting into.

Relax

Easier said than done. But remembering the basics will help. Like . . . don't forget to breathe. Maintain eye contact with members of your audience. If there is a friendly face out there, return to that person a few times over the course of your presentation. Stand up straight, it will help with your breathing and it will make you come across as confident and comfortable.

Modern Etiquette

Phone Manners: Hello?

Every time anyone (you or anyone working for you) picks up the phone, she should announce your company's name.

If you work from home, install a separate business line, so your two-year-old doesn't pick up calls from clients.

Instead of call-waiting, install at least one rollover line or a voice mailbox through your phone company.

If you need to put a client on hold, a brief but polite sentence such as, "Would you mind if I put you on hold for a moment?" works better than the telephone-operator-sounding "please hold."

Don't let the phone ring too many times. When setting up your mailbox, arrange it so the phone rings only two or three times. It is frustrating to be sitting on the other end of the line listening to ring after ring.

If a three-way conference call is necessary, find out how to do it before the call is scheduled. Disconnecting a client because you are unfamiliar with the telephone's features isn't very professional. The good news is that there are loads of free conference call services, so setting up the call is easy and cheap.

E-mails, E-mails, E-mails

A great deal of communication is done by e-mail these days. This is a positive because you can get so much done in such a brief amount of time.

Use the time zones to your advantage

If you are doing business across many time zones, e-mail is the only way to go. We do some business with an Australian production company, and there is only one hour a day when we are both in the office at the same time. It's much easier to send an e-mail and get the reply the next day than to try to make contact during that one hour.

Don't forget confirmation of receipt

When the information you are e-mailing about is important (as in, it is the kind of information that will require you to cover your butt should there be a problem), ask for a confirmation of receipt. Either set it up through your e-mail system or ask your recipient to confirm with you.

Keep it positive

Never e-mail complaints or criticisms. You can't control the tone of your e-mail, and if someone is feeling defensive, the words might come across as much harsher than you intended. Have conversations of this nature in person or on the phone. While it may be easier to express anger at someone by e-mail, it is never as effective as discussing something in person. Never, ever complain or criticize a third party via e-mail. You have zero control over where your e-mails go once they are sent; so again, do it by phone or in person. Last, don't e-mail in place of a confrontation you are avoiding. Talking is always best, and e-mails can be ignored or deleted if they are unpleasant in nature.

HOW TO PROTECT YOURSELF
IN THE WILD WORLD OF E-MAIL

E-mail is the most convenient and dangerous invention ever created. You can gossip on the phone with half the world and not do the kind of damage one bitchy word in an e-mail can do. Hell, if someone calls you complaining about the gossip, chances are the story this person heard isn't the one you were telling and you can deny it. There's no denying the black-and-white e-mail. Never ever e-mail anything that you would feel uncomfortable about if even one other person saw it. So in the true "Cover Your Ass" entrepreneurial spirit that is required in these competitive times, we offer you some e-mail don'ts.

DON'T just blindly forward material along. Always read from the bottom and delete anything that may compromise someone else. You've got to protect one another.

DON'T forget to read from the bottom up when people forward e-mails around. Most people forget that a trail of information is included and, more times than not, not meant for you to see. We've actually been forwarded correspondence from clients sharing inter-departmental haggling about our fee. We're quite sure we weren't meant to see that.

DON'T forward junk mail or chain letters. Ever. It's just a pain in the ass, and if you become known for them, people stop reading anything you send.

DON'T mark them *urgent* if they aren't. Most people are getting fifty-plus e-mails a day and need to prioritize them. If you need immediate action, pick up the phone.

DON'T forget to check who is actually in the "To" line. Because of auto-fill, it's all too easy to send things to the wrong person. Your client doesn't need to know that you're fighting with your husband.

DON'T ever confuse the "reply" and "reply to all" key.

DON'T ever delete an e-mail. The electronic trail is the greatest thing about it. Create folders and file e-mails for future use.

DON'T use those stupid smiley faces ☺ or TXTing shorthand. It's just irritating.

DO check out the book *Send: Why People E-Mail So Badly and How to Do It Better* (revised edition), by David Shipley and Will Schwalbe.

Handling Confrontation as an Adult: We'll See about That!

Confrontation as a new business owner can often feel as shaming as a reprimand from your sixth-grade teacher. When a customer yells at you because you broke an item while bagging it or an employee is furious at her new schedule and so decides to scream, you can be reduced to tears almost instantaneously. You have to learn how to deal with situations like this, because when you own a business, the occasional conflict will arise.

Everyone we interviewed for this book said that learning how to manage confrontations with confidence and grace was one of the most rewarding benefits of being an entrepreneur. Chris Wolfer, of Construction Information Systems, shares that "learning how to see yourself as equal to your clients and having enough confidence in your work to stand up for yourself during a conflict is not only the most difficult part of being an entrepreneur, but is actually the only worthwhile experience you will take from your whole career."

The good news about conflict is that as a business owner, the tone of any professional confrontation is really up to you, because you are dealing with either someone you pay or someone who pays you.

When you are the one confronting someone with a problem, try to keep your talking points professional, and keep the name-calling to a minimum. You want to be clear with them about exactly what the problem is and how you would like to have it solved. By providing a solution, you have made it easy for them to address (and fix) the issue. If you are unhappy with your bookkeeper—maybe she has made just one too many mistakes—ask her to come in and meet with you. Offer specific examples of errors she has made. If you are going to give her another chance, spell out the parameters of the arrangement—such as, you will keep working with her, but if there is one more inaccuracy, she will be fired. If you run a cleaning business and a client isn't paying you on time, place a phone call to remind the person of your payment policy. If the client keeps at it, then you might want to set up a system with this client whereby you are paid ahead for the work. If your phone bill was inaccurate, call the business customer service department and outline for them the billing issues you have; offer to fax them a copy of your statement; and emphasize what a good customer you are and how you would like to stay with them (they will be extra helpful if they think you are going to take your business elsewhere).

When you are confronted by someone, don't take it personally. Listen to what is being said and, employing a successful therapy technique, repeat back to them what they told you so that they know you are hearing them. If they resort to name-calling, either end the conversation or rise above it—you might even laugh about it later. We were recently called "divas" by a client we fired for reasons too boring to go into here (hint: he was mean). We got a lot of mileage out of that insult. For months afterward while we were packing boxes, licking envelopes for invitations, sprinting to the post office before it closed, we would laugh about being divas. We wish.

Quick Tips for Managing a Confrontation

Don't take it personally
That doesn't mean that you shouldn't listen or that maybe you weren't in error. It means that it isn't about you as a person; at the most, it is about decisions you have made as a business owner.

Get everything in writing

And we mean everything. Contracts with vendors, leases, project agreements with clients, receipts for clients. It will minimize problems down the road if you have something to show.

Do it in person or on the phone

If you have a problem with a vendor, client, or customer, discuss it in person or at the very least over the phone. Don't do it by e-mail, and try not to write letters unless you are establishing a paper trail. People will respect you more if you deal with them directly.

Admit when you are in the wrong

Repeat back to the angry party exactly what her issues with you are. If you are in the wrong, acknowledge it immediately (if you own a customer service business, you will be admitting you are wrong more often than many other professions, in order to keep your customers happy), and either offer a solution or tell her that you will be getting back to her with a solution in the very near future.

| girl talk | **Caitlin's Story** |

As the cofounder of YC Media and the coauthor of the *Girl's Guide* series, Caitlin spent years thinking about and writing about women at work. Yet while she was giving advice all over the world about how to create a professional life that fits one's personal passions and responsibilities, she just couldn't seem to manage that for herself. In fact, as her twins were getting older and the to-do list was growing longer, she was decidedly drowning. As it was for many people, the shifting economy was her wake-up call. To be fair to her business and writing partner, Kim, and to make more money, she would either have to put more energy and time into YC Media or reconfigure her life. After a long, hard, honest look in the mirror, she admitted to herself that PR was not her personal passion and that as much as she loved being in business with Kim she wanted to put her energy toward writing. And take it from her, being a freelance writer is starting your own business.

Following much of the advice in this book, Caitlin began laying the groundwork to open Caitlin, Inc. To prepare for the change, the first thing she did was have a sit-down with her husband to review the budget. She needed to know how much she would need to bring in each month and if there was any time for her to ramp up. Big surprise, there was minimal cushion to ramp up so it was important to reduce expenses while lining up some work. The Friedmans had recently moved to Brooklyn from Manhattan, so luckily they were already spending far less. As for the income, fortuitously, a part-time managing editor job fell out of the sky. After interviewing and submitting writing samples, Caitlin was offered the job to create and manage content for *beyondmotherhood.com* (a site to help moms figure out if, when, and how to get back to work). The part-time job was a fraction of her previous income but it required only a twenty-five hour-a-week commitment, giving Caitlin time to work on the writing projects that she had neglected for too long.

Then there was the incorporating part. This time she registered her business as an S Corporation. The process was fast and easy with *legalzoom.com*, but it's important if you go this route to make sure you have an accountant help you with registering the tax paperwork with city, state, and federal departments. Without YC Media, the Friedmans didn't have health insurance, so researching options and obtaining it was the next thing on the list, followed by new bank accounts and a corporate credit card to help track expenses. She set up a receipt file for the new freelance business, organized vendor files, and bought a new BlackBerry. She had her IT guy, Frank, work with her to figure out an e-mail-contact-calendar system that would be effective but also really cheap.

Making sure there was a plan on the writing front too, Caitlin created a project timeline to follow, scheduling blocks of time during the week for her to actually do the writing she left her job for.

So after a graceful dissolution of the partnership and managing all of the small and large details that make the foundation of starting a business, Caitlin moved home and set up shop at the dining room table. Now she can honestly say that her work life is in harmony with her personal life and that things are good.

8

The Girl's Guide to Surviving Today's Technology

In our partnership, we had split the time-consuming responsibilities. One of us handled the money, and the other dealt with all things technological. Techno partner loves shiny new toys. She was the first one on her block to have DSL and annually upgrades her computer. At prior jobs, she always volunteered to be the in-house IT contact and database manager. She considered herself pretty savvy in the world of computers and new technologies. What we realized the hard way was she knew just enough to be dangerous. Learn from our mistakes. In this chapter we offer you the "book within the book," a technology survival-guide based on our real-life near-computer-death experiences and a combined history of four hundred logged hours of technical support.

What does a girl really need to set up shop? Actually, not as much as you might think—reliable phone service with voice mail, cellular phone service, and a decent computer with a suite of software that offers word processing, accounting, contact management, and e-mail, as well as high-speed Internet access. We break it all down for you here.

Can You Hear Us Now?

The phone is your most basic piece of communication equipment. For those who are always on the go, you've got it the easiest. Sign up with the cellular service that has the best coverage in your area—carefully review those maps. Buy the most minutes you can and all the features— voice mail, caller ID, text messaging, data and Internet access—and get down to business. Reliable phone service is a priority for any business and not the place to skimp. Resist the urge to cancel your landline.

Should You Buy Feature Phones or Invest in a Phone System?

Multifeature phones are the stand-alone phones you have at home. They cost from $30 to $500, and you can buy them from any office supply store. Some feature phones can be linked together to create mini phone systems. Key features for a new business setup include multiple lines, automatic redial, speakerphone, headset jack, caller ID, autoattendant (a computer that answers and transfers to an extension), and conference and call-transfer capabilities. Generally, you buy and program feature phones yourself—saving additional consultant fees. We recommend purchasing multiline feature phones if you are fewer than four people, plan to answer your own phones, and have no plans to increase your head count within the first two years. We went to an office supply store and purchased three four-line feature phones for $199 each and installed and programmed them ourselves. The phones work fine, but the built-in answering machine is truly horrible. YC Media now uses Volp phone system and Skype (without video) whenever possible to save money.

A computerized phone system is a setup of phones and voice mail operated by a personal computer. They have to be installed, set up, and maintained by an outside vendor, and they cost anywhere from $1,000 to $5,000 for entry-level systems and from $5,000 to $50,000 for more advanced ones. We recently got two quotes for new phone systems— both were for four lines with voice mail and expandable up to twenty lines. The systems each had a voice-prompt answering system and caller directory. One quote was for $2,200 plus a phone purchase price of $565. The other was $3,500. We didn't even ask about the phone price. One of the cooler features of the phone system for many small businesses is that when a call comes in, a caller ID window pops up on your computer screen. The window is connected to a database that provides a whole bunch of information about the caller: last time they called, status of project, as well as all of their contact details. You can take notes right in the call window and automatically have a detailed log of all calls received. Our phone consultant (oh, yeah, we now have a phone consultant in addition to our computer consultant, attorney, accountant, and bookkeeper—and we're a low-overhead operation!) advised us to shop around as one of the benefits of the crashed economy is that businesses are selling off their systems on eBay and Craig'slist.

Where Should You Get Landline Phone Service?

Order your phone service from the oldest, biggest, most reliable provider in your area—no matter what the cost. In the early stages of your business you need reliability and peace of mind much more than you need an extra $20 per month. The telecommunications industry is just too volatile to go with a newcomer. We learned this the hard way.

Just after we signed our office lease, we asked our landlord if he'd recommend his phone service. We didn't think we had the time or expertise to do an analysis of our options. We figured that some old guy with forty years of experience in the business world must have done his homework. Nope. It turns out that he chose Teligent (now a bankrupt phone company) because he was in dispute and angry with Verizon. He eventually skipped the country, and we still see unpaid Verizon bills coming to the office. Lessons from this scenario: (1) unless you really check out somebody and their business, don't assume they know anything more than you; (2) take the time to do the research yourself even if you don't want to; (3) just because they are older and male doesn't mean they know anything.

Should You Order Residential or Business Service?

Order business phone lines. It's tempting to order residential service because it's cheaper than business—sometimes by as much as 50 percent. Business lines are worth the money because they come with guaranteed same-day service calls—and the technician must stay until the problem is fixed. If you have residential lines and they go out, you could wait as many as three days for service. Phone service providers are now offering small business packages with a suite of services (such as call forwarding, caller ID, and voice mail) that makes the price even easier to stomach.

Long Distance or Internet Telephony?

Long distance service is the one area where it's worth shopping around. Small, low-cost long distance providers purchase huge blocks of long distance service at very low rates, then sell the minutes back to you at lower rates than you can get from major carriers. They also offer calling cards and 800 numbers at reduced rates. The easiest way to do a comparison is to go to *www.smartprice.com* or *www.saveonphone.com*. They don't require releasing private information or a commitment. To qualify for the lowest rates, you must be willing to pay automatically every month with a credit card. The next wave in low-cost long distance service is Internet phone calling, and Skype.

Voice Over IP (VoIP), Internet Telephony, IP Telephony, iTelephony, and Skype

No more sending phone calls over copper wire. Now the process of routing calls over the Internet goes by any of these names. At the moment the terminology and the technology are quite confusing. Bottom line: There are four ways you could talk to someone using VoIP. According to *www.howstuffworks.com*, "If you've got a computer or a telephone, you can use at least one of these methods without buying any new equipment."

Computer-to-computer—Most instant-messaging programs offer a chatting option where the other party must be on-line to receive this "call" through the computer. You use a speaker and microphone, and other than free long distance, there are no advantages for small businesses.

Computer-to-telephone—You can call anyone who has a phone from your computer (with the microphone and speaker setup), and you need a free software download such as Skype, which offers free phone calls and videoconferencing.

Telephone-to-computer—Zero practical small business application, as far as we can see.

Telephone-to-telephone—Sign up with a VoIP provider and it works the same way e-mail does except voice is transmitted over the Internet instead of text. Start-up is expensive because you have to buy phones and a router, and have it all installed and maintained. The long distance savings over time should make up for it, though.

BlackBerry versus iPhone 3G

BlackBerry was created with business use in mind. It runs on a Microsoft Exchange server and automatically syncs e-mail with your desktop. It works seamlessly anywhere around the world (based on your service plan). It makes reliable phone calls (again, based on your service plan) and can take photos and surf the web, albeit slowly. It plays no games, unless you're a Brickbreaker fanatic, and should be used for e-mail, phone calls, and Facebook updates.

Apple's iPhone was created for fun. Syncing e-mail is more of a process, and the AT&T network on which it runs provides unreliable service. And you have to type on a screen that is difficult to get used to after using a QWERTY keyboard. But what fun you can have: games, music, and the plethora of apps available make the iPhone a winner for personal use. We're just not sure your evening bag can carry both!

The Search for the Right Computer

Purchasing a computer can be overwhelming and confusing (add it to the ever-growing list). There are thousands of configurations, a number of big and reliable manufactures (not to mention the Mac versus PC question), and too many retail, catalog, and on-line outlets to even begin to comparison shop.

We recommend you get help when purchasing your first business computer. An IT (information technologies) consultant is an absolute must-hire. Unless computers are your core business, you probably won't have the expertise to purchase and install things correctly. And you shouldn't even want to. Keep your eye on the prize: starting up a successful business. Learning how to build networks isn't on your core competencies list. Sure, go ahead and add that new printer to your system. But always hire a professional to set you up right—right out of the gate. A good consultant will become an integral part of your small business team and help you plan and budget for your future growth. Your IT consultant is a lot more valuable if she can integrate all your systems: phone, computers, networks, and high-speed Internet service, and the easiest way to find a good one is to ask other business owners, especially those in your field. After you get recommendations, interview the candidates and ask for additional references. Make sure you call the references.

Little tip: Never, ever be the first on your block when it comes to technology. The new, colorful, and exciting stuff hot off the production line never works—and the technical support guys will even admit it if you keep them on the phone long enough. Wait for the second or third round of designs. They will be cheaper, work better, and the technical support teams will have seen enough problems to be able to troubleshoot quickly.

Questions to Ask When Interviewing Computer Consultants

What kinds of businesses do you work with?

What sizes of businesses do you work with?

Are you a PC or Mac specialist?

We are a start-up. How do you figure out what we need? Can you help us create an infrastructure that will grow with us?

Can you make recommendations and set up all of our Internet needs, including web-hosting, exchange servers, and e-mail hosting?

How do you bill?

If we have problems during off-hours, how can we reach you? And is there an increase in your rate at those times?

Can you help us find inexpensive or refurbished equipment? What if we need to lease our equipment?

Will you interface with our telephone consultant to set up our Internet connection?

Do you have expertise in networks and networking?

Do you have experience with remote-access setups?

Can you help us with software?

Do you make recommendations for PDAs, BlackBerrys, and iPhones?

| the word | **Frank Vasquez**
Saber Technology |

Yes, Frank is a man, and the only one in the book. He is our computer consultant and all-around lifesaver. When the computer crashes, we call Frank. When the Internet connection goes down, we call Frank. When we don't know who else to call, we call Frank. So when we couldn't find a woman consultant (and believe us, we searched), we called Frank. Here he offers advice about four important things to consider when setting up your new office.

Web presence and connectivity: How will you get on-line (DSL, cable, T1)? Do you want to have your own domain name, which will allow you to have an e-mail address like *email@yourcompany.com*, or do you want e-mail sent to *yourcompany@gmail.com* or *yourcompany@yahoo.com*? Are you going to develop a web site or blog? You can own a domain name without the additional expense of developing a web site, so you can protect your company name and use the e-mail address.

Network: How will you connect the computers? Where will you place the wiring? Wireless networking is an option but not recommended, because it is still more susceptible to failure and security issues. Do you need a file server, or is sharing a user workstation enough? Save money by buying heavy-duty printers that can be shared over your network.

Workstations: How fast do you want your computers to be? Don't buy the cheapest PC available. It will probably cost you more in downtime and headaches in the long run. Nor do you want the best money can buy, since that is usually overpriced. A PC that has been released for about six months has the best cost-to-functionality ratio and will last about three years.

Data backup: You must have a backup up of your most critical data. There are inexpensive external hard drives that can be used as removable backup devices. Or you can subscribe to an on-line backup service like Carbonite (*www.carbonite.com*).

Computers 101

When you start comparing machines, it becomes apparent that there are certain basic computer components that are always part of the package, and you should understand the terms that describe them.

CPU: The *central processing unit*, where the speed is. Also called the *microprocessor,* it's measured in megahertz.

RAM: *Random access memory*, and bigger is better. RAM is measured in megabytes.

DRIVES: floppy, Zip, CD-RW, or CD-DVD. These all run disks that information can be "written" onto.

PORTS: USB, SCSI, parallel, serial—the connectors for peripherals such as printers, scanners, PDAs, Zip drives, cameras, and mp3s.

MONITORS: CRT, LCD, plasma, touch screen, TV, and cable-ready. Monitors come in all shapes and prices. Be sure to check out the dot pitch. The higher the pitch, the less sharp the picture is. And blurry pictures give girls a headache.

VIDEO AND SOUND CARDS: VGA and SVGA refer to *video cards*, and cool-named things like "Sound Blaster 512 PCI" are *sound cards*. They make great audio for games, movies, and music.

ETHERNET CONNECTION: The wide jack on the computer that looks like a phone jack and is used to plug into a network.

Keyboard/mouse: Pretty self-explanatory, but now they have wireless ones that work great. Reducing the number of cords on your computer is a good thing, because all too quickly they become an unsightly mess.

Warranties, Rebates, Tech-Support, and Repairs

Every once in a while, computers, like cars (and men), are lemons. Make sure when you purchase any piece of computer equipment that you investigate the warranty and register for it. Most manufacturers attach an identification code to your computer that identifies you (and your tech-support privileges) to the technical support team.

Networks and Networking

Networks are built to connect computers and share files. They can be wired or wireless. Files can be stored on a file server or on a host computer. We're going to explain the major components of a network so you can have an intelligent conversation with your consultant. The prices for networking are continually coming down, so plan for a network that can be inexpensively and regularly upgraded.

We've been in business for three years and have upgraded our network twice. We share a printer, added a firewall ($499) in year two for increased security, and have already used two different routers (we explain them, along with other network terms, next) because we changed our Internet providers twice.

The Network Scoop

Local area networks (LAN): Connect many devices that are relatively close to one another, usually in the same building. *Wide area networks* (WAN) connect (with wires leased from the local telephone company) a larger number of devices, usually two or more LANs. LANs are generally faster.

Routers: Used to connect devices around the world as part of the global Internet. Your DSL or T1 line (see Reliable High-Speed Internet Access, which follows) is connected to a router, which traffics information between the Internet and your computer. Your router is connected to your firewall.

FIREWALLS: Protect your network from evil outside forces and viruses. A firewall is hardware and software. The hardware is a little device that plugs into your network line, and the software comes in the form of subscriptions for virus protection. We use a SonicWALL hardware firewall. It's one of those things that protect us and we don't have to worry about it, so we like it.

Reliable High-Speed Internet Access

INTERNET SERVICE PROVIDERS (ISPs): ISPs connect you to the Internet for a fee. Most businesses require high-speed (bigger bandwidth) access. You can get high-speed access from DSL, cable modems, satellite Internet, or a T1 line. We'll explain them to you. Like Internet telephony, this stuff is changing every day. Do your homework on reliable carriers and try to speak with someone else who actually uses the technology. Phone service providers are also into the DSL, FiOS, and T1 business, so ask about package prices.

DSL (DIGITAL SUBSCRIBER LINE): A standard telephone installation in the United States consists of a plastic-covered pair of copper wires that the phone company installs in your home. The copper wires have lots of room for carrying more than your phone conversations. DSL carries information on the wire without disturbing the line's ability to carry conversations. The entire plan is based on matching particular frequencies to specific tasks. Modern equipment that sends digital rather than analog data can safely use much more of the telephone line's capacity.

Most homes and small business users are connected to an asymmetric DSL (ADSL) line. ADSL divides up the available frequencies in a line on the assumption that most Internet users look at, or download, much more information than they send, or upload. Under this assumption, if the connection speed from the Internet to the user is three to four times faster than the connection from the user back to the

Internet, then the user will see the most benefit most of the time. ADSL is a distance-sensitive technology: As the connection's length increases, the signal quality decreases and the connection speed goes down.

CABLE MODEMS: Cable modems also capitalize on their extra bandwidth. Each television signal is given a 6-megahertz channel on the cable. The coaxial cable used to carry cable television can carry hundreds of megahertz of signals. When a cable TV company offers Internet access, Internet information can use that same cable because the cable modem system puts the data sent from the Internet to an individual computer into its own 6 megahertz channel. Upstream data—information sent from an individual back to the Internet—requires just 2 megahertz, so it all fits quite nicely.

SATELLITE INTERNET: Two-way satellite Internet consists of a two-foot-by-three-foot dish, two modems (uplink and downlink), and coaxial cables between the dish and modem. The key installation-planning requirement is a clear view to the south, since the orbiting satellites are over the equator area. And as with satellite TV, trees and heavy rains can affect reception of the Internet signals.

FIBER OPTICS (AKA FIOS): FiOS is a unique technology currently offered by Verizon nationally that transmits data through hair-thin strands of glass fiber, using laser-generated pulses of light. This yields mind-boggling speed, almost no loss of quality over long distances, and virtually unlimited capacity, or "bandwidth." FiOS is not available everywhere yet, but it is a cost-effective solution for all of your communication (television, phone, and Internet) needs.

T1 LINES: T1 lines are usually fiber-optic lines, installed by the phone company (although they also come in copper). A T1 line can carry twenty-four digitized voice channels. If the T1 line is being used for telephone conversations, it plugs into the office's phone system. If it is carrying data, it plugs into the network's router. A T1 line might cost between

$1,000 and $1,500 per month, depending on who provides it and where it goes. The other end of the T1 line needs to be connected to an ISP, and the total cost is a combination of the fee the phone company charges and the fee the ISP charges.

The Operating System

Most manufacturers choose the operating system for you. Generally, PC-based machines operate on Microsoft Windows XP. Macintosh includes the updated version of their own operating system on all new machines. Unix/Linux is an open-code operating system that is becoming more popular for large businesses in reaction to Microsoft's monopoly.

Office Productivity Software

A computer doesn't do anything without the software programs telling it what to do. As with the operating system, most computer manufacturers bundle (preload) a suite of software onto the computer for your use. The manufacturers of the most widely available software are Corel, Lotus Development, and, of course, Microsoft. Software suites include word processing, spreadsheets, e-mail, desktop publishing, presentation, and database applications. For a minor difference in price, you can upgrade to the "professional" versions of these applications that offer more features.

If you have any experience with menu-driven applications, you can learn to use the programs. If you have no experience at all, the programs come with detailed tutorials. What can be frustrating, though, is that no software comes with manuals anymore. All the manuals are on-line and need to be downloaded from the manufacturer's web site.

We recommend you purchase your bookkeeper's preferred accounting package. We use QuickBooks Pro, and although it takes a little time to get up and running because of the information for each client that needs to be input, once it gets going it's very easy to manage.

Databases can be a big deal if you design them from scratch. We recommend that, wherever possible, you investigate "out-of-the-box" programs that are designed for your specific needs. There is something for everyone out there. Manage a sales force? Look into GoldMine contact management software. It's designed to automate sales-force tasks, maintain one main database, and communicate with all the team members. All you (the end user) do is enter data. Many industries have proprietary software too. For example, you can buy a restaurant package that incorporates all the business of the restaurant, from taking reservations to ordering meat from your purveyor.

TEN TIPS TO DE-STRESS IN SIXTY MINUTES OR LESS

The computer crashed, it's raining, the phones are down, your deadline has passed, and you want to scream. What's a girl to do to blow off a little steam?

1. **Mani-pedi:** Getting a manicure and pedicure is a great way to relax for an hour or so. Not only do you get a mini hand-and-foot massage, you spend the next week smiling down at your pretty hands and feet.

2. **Exercise:** We know everybody tells you that exercise, yoga, Pilates, boxing, and so on, will cure what ails you. But you hate to exercise. Skip on down to number three.

3. **Spend some money:** Go out to lunch. Get a makeover. Buy a new blouse or a bouquet of flowers. A tiny purchase is always a pick-me-up.

4. **Call a friend and gossip:** You've been working so hard since you started up your business, sometimes it's just nice to chat for fifteen minutes. Of course if you're stressed because your phones went out, move on.

5. **Daydream about faraway places:** Check out airfares to Hawaii or Paris on *www.hotwire.com*. Look at newspapers from other cities. Surf around and see what's happening someplace else.

---

6. **Read gossip columns and check out celebrity photos:** Celebrity gossip is a great way to take your mind off your problems; check out *www.pagesix.com* or *TMZ*.

7. **Shop on-line:** Differs from spending money because you have the full sixty minutes to shop—no time wasted walking to the store.

8. **Read the newspaper:** Scan the pages you wouldn't normally have time for and broaden your horizons.

9. **Make your social plans for the weekend:** Check out the movie listings, gallery shows, free concerts, new restaurants, or book readings for the upcoming weekend.

10. **Hobby time:** Pull out your knitting, needlepoint, or trashy novel, and get your mind off your anxieties.

girl talk

Larissa Kisielewska, Founder
Optimum Design and Consulting

Optimum Design and Consulting combines fresh design talent and experienced production professionals with Macintosh computer technology experts. All of Lara's clients are committed Mac users. The firm focuses on electronic publishing. They offer Mac-based IT consulting in addition to design, printing, and prepress services. The company is certified by the New York State Department of Economic Development as a Woman-Owned Business Enterprise. Lara shared her Mac experience with us and provided some guidance on the great Mac-versus-PC debate.

What questions should you answer when starting from scratch?
What type of business will you have? How many users? What are the main uses of the computer? Will you be hosting large database files or web sites? Do you have multiple offices in

different locations? What are the sizes of the offices? Are you doing your own accounting? How much information needs to be shared among staff? Will you want to track sales, clients, inventory? What else needs to be tracked? What kind of budget should you be thinking about?

What businesses are better for Macs, which for PC? What are the main differences?
Traditionally, graphics people have used Macs because of the better high-end print production software and hardware available, better resolution of the monitors, and ease of use when sharing files with other users in the industry, who are also using Macs. Other markets that tend to favor Macs are education (for ease of use with the Mac's graphical interface) and sciences (for the Mac's longtime high-end graphics capability). Everything PCs can do, Macs can also do; so everyday applications, such as databases, spreadsheets, accounting, word processing, and Internet access, can be done on either platform with little or no difference. Today which computer you use has almost solely to do with personal preference, since you can use both to accomplish the same tasks.

Do you make software recommendations too? Say a customer needs a new database, how do you help them evaluate which one would be best for them?
We would ask the following questions: What do they need to track? Do they need multiuser access? How many users? Do they need the capability to publish data on the Internet? Do they need remote access? What is the approximate size of the data files? Where are the files going to be stored?

Let's talk about web sites. Do you have a favorite host service? Your company also designs web sites. What kind

**of budgets should start-ups consider when putting a new
site up? What are the variables to consider?**

We don't have a favorite host service; most of them offer similar services at similar rates. When putting up a new site, the
variables to consider are: Is your site purely informational (like a
brochure about your company), or will it be interactive? What is
your target audience, and what would they be looking for from
your site? Do you want to have password-protection to access
certain parts of the site? If you want people to think of your site
as a resource, what kind of information will it have? If you want
people to return to your site periodically, what kind of new information will you put up? How often will it change? How will people know that it has changed? Are you aiming to collect data
about the people who view your site? If so, what kind of reward
will you give them for entering their data into your form? Will
you need to sell anything over your site? If so, how secure do
you need your site to be? Do you need an intranet component
for your site so that your employees or partner companies can
access private parts of the site? What kind of viewer statistics
do you want to track?

Sites range from $500 to $25,000, depending on how
large they are and what kind of complexity and programming
are needed. Most sites we do for start-ups are in the $1,500- to
$2,500-range.

**How do you recommend clients plan for growth? For
example, a file server can be expensive. What are low-cost
options for small networks?**

If the client believes they will expand in the near future, it is
cheaper overall to put basic measures in place to allow for
expansion. For example, if computers will be added later on,
the client should construct a network that can easily be added
to instead of one that will serve only a few computers and would

have to be completely redone with additional expansion. Mac networks do not necessarily need a server unless they are very large. Any Mac can act as a server for other computers on the same network, so the cost of a server will be the same as that of any other desktop machine. An existing machine can easily be configured to be used as a server. Configuration of the computers on a server-based network is relatively straightforward, so small Mac networks are very cheap to set up, including wiring, a hub to route network traffic through, and labor.

What is the most important advice you can offer a Mac owner dealing with a world of PC-based technology?
There are solutions for virtually every issue a Mac user may encounter. You just may need to dig a little (or ask a Mac consultant) to find the answers. Owning a Mac can give a client the best of both worlds—Apple developers take into account the fact that the PC has the main market share and thus develop most products to work equally on both platforms.

9

A Girl's Gotta Write
Proposals, Presentations, and Other Business Writing

Business writing is a formal and important means of expression. When done right, a new-business letter or well-worded business proposal will win a client. When poorly executed, it will lose the client and create bad word of mouth. This chapter will offer examples for everything you need, including the keys to hosting an effective brainstorming session, tips for what to include in a new-client proposal, and a business inquiry letter that will get you a meeting.

The ability to communicate effectively through writing should never be taken for granted. Writing is tough—plain and simple. It is, however, a craft that can be learned and improved with practice. No matter what business you have chosen, you will have to communicate with somebody (customers, clients, vendors, colleagues, or employees) in writing. There are many books devoted to business writing (we own a copy of *The Complete Idiot's Guide to Terrific Business Writing*, from Alpha Books).

For many of your professional interactions, a piece of writing will be your first introduction to a potential client. Whether responding to a formal request for a proposal or simply sending an introductory e-mail to someone you met at a party, the words you put down will be the foundation for all future communication.

But before we get to the words, let's take a step back and examine the ideas behind the words. How do you generate a good idea? And what about a *great* idea? A good place to start is with a brainstorming session.

Put Your Thinking Caps On: The Keys to an Effective Brainstorming Session

Brainstorming is an excellent way of developing many creative solutions to a problem. Focus on a problem and then generate as many radical solutions as you can. Ideas should deliberately be as broad and odd as possible, and they should be developed as fast as possible. Brainstorming is a lateral-thinking process; it is designed to help you break out of habitual thinking patterns and into new ways of looking at things.

During brainstorming sessions, there should be no criticism of ideas—you are trying to open possibilities and break down wrong assumptions about the limits of the solution.

Evaluate your ideas after the brainstorming session has finished. Then explore your solutions in detail.

When you brainstorm on your own, you tend to produce a wider range of ideas than during group brainstorming. There's no need to worry about other people's egos or opinions, so you can be more creative. However, you may be someone who's not able to develop ideas sitting alone in a room, so you may want to gather a group.

Assembling a group for brainstorming can be very effective. Group brainstorming uses the experience and creativity of all members of the group. When individual members reach their limit on an idea, another member's creativity and experience can take the idea to the next level. Group brainstorming tends to develop ideas in more depth than individual brainstorming.

Brainstorming in a group can be risky for some individuals. Valuable but strange suggestions may appear stupid at first sight. The brainstorming leader needs to make sure that the naysayers don't crush these ideas and humiliate other group members.

Participants in the brainstorming process should come from as wide a range of disciplines as possible. This brings a broad range of experience to the session and helps to make it more creative.

We'll begin with a sample memo inviting the team from a retail store to a brainstorming session for the forthcoming holiday season.

Date: March 20
To: All employees of Harried Hobby House
From: Hannah Harry, Owner
Re: Holiday Hobby Brainstorm

Hi Guys,

It's time for the annual Holiday Hobby Brainstorming Session. Last year's sales were a bit soft, and this year we're hoping to get a boost from an integrated catalog and retail-themed promotion. So we're looking for the great ideas.

I'll bring the bagels and coffee if you all will come in 30 minutes before opening next Thursday, March 27. Our goal is to generate 10 exciting holiday themes that we can use to merchandise the store and our catalog.

There are no bad ideas. Come with everything you've got, and if possible, talk to your friends and family and bring their input too.

We'll cover the walls with our ideas, and by the time we open, we should be able to edit them down to our top 10.

The winning idea will be awarded a $50 cash prize. Put your thinking caps on, and we'll see you next week.

Brainstorming Checklist

SET A CLEAR AND SPECIFIC OBJECTIVE FOR YOUR BRAINSTORMING SESSION AND PROVIDE BACKGROUND INFORMATION SO PEOPLE CAN COME PREPARED. Make your goals as specific as possible. "Ten new themes for the holiday season" is pretty clear. You want attendees to come to the meeting armed with ideas. If you are inviting folks who aren't familiar with your business or project, provide a couple of background paragraphs for them.

ASSEMBLE A DIVERSE GROUP. Many times the best ideas come from those who aren't experienced (or jaded) enough to edit themselves. Put the squeeze on your friends, family, or colleagues for their input.

CLICHÉD BUT TRUE: THERE ARE NO BAD IDEAS. The goal here is to get as many ideas as possible on paper without any filter. At the end of the meeting, the group will weed out the good from the bad, but the process should be free and open. As a new business owner, you are so close to everything that it's sometimes difficult to get perspective on good ideas, so don't reject anything until you've explored it in more detail.

SET A TIME LIMIT, AND STICK TO IT. Invite the group for thirty minutes or even fifteen. The worst thing you can do is go at it for a long time. There should be a lot of energy in the room, and most people run out of gas after thirty minutes.

WRITE DOWN ALL IDEAS. Assign someone to take the minutes and record everything. An effective way of recording the ideas is to write them on big sheets of paper tacked to the wall—that way everyone can see what's been said. After the meeting, assign someone to transcribe what's on the big sheets.

PROVIDE INCENTIVES. Generally, you need to assemble more people than you have on staff. In the case of the retail example, you're asking your employees to come in early (or on their day off), and their efforts should be acknowledged. This is not their company or store. In our hobby-store scenario, management provided breakfast and a cash prize. If you are asking friends, or putting the word out on Facebook, make sure you at least offer refreshments. (One of the perks of being product publicists is that we always have a book, a pan, or a bottle or two of olive oil lying around for a goodie bag.)

COMMUNICATE THE RESULTS. After a brainstorming session, it is important to deliver the results either in a memo to the group or incorporated into a bigger document. The last thing you want to do is get a bunch of people together for their ideas and then not do anything with them.

Business Letters for All Occasions

No matter what type of business letter you are writing (see the sample that follows), they all share a similar structure: introduction, body, and conclusion. Your *introduction* clearly states who you are and what you want in one or two paragraphs. Few people take the time to read beyond a rambling or vague opening. Remember, this is not a creative-writing exercise but a call to action. The *body* provides the details and supporting evidence for your introduction. The *conclusion* summarizes your letter and provides that call to action.

Keep your letters to one page. Few people have the time or interest to read more than that. With the barrage of e-mails that people receive daily, a letter that is printed out, signed, stuffed in an envelope, stamped, and dropped in the mail, automatically identifies itself as important. Make sure you deliver.

I've Got the Goods:
Writing an Effective Business-Pitch Letter

As publicists, we write pitch letters all the time. Our letters seek to generate media placement for our clients, but their structure is similar to any other pitch letter. We've included one for review.

Dear [insert name],

If you asked an American to choose between a plate of pesticides and chemical additives or a simple dish of grilled vegetables with pasta, most would look at you as if you were insane and choose the pasta. And yet that's exactly what we do every time we eat fast food or heat up chicken nuggets for dinner. As a country, we've lost touch with our food—so much so that the First Lady of the United States planted a garden at the White House so that schoolchildren would understand where vegetables come from. It's time to make better choices, and a new cookbook from a new voice in food will show us how.

"The cleaner we eat, the clearer we think, and the better we can embrace good health and nutrition," writes Terry Walters in her debut cookbook, **CLEAN FOOD: A Seasonal Guide to Eating Close to the Source (Sterling Epicure, September 15, 2009; $30.00/hardcover.)** "If you can read or imagine how it grows, it's clean. If you can't, neither can your body. You're better off without!"

Terry teaches us how to eat clean (and by the way, clean is green too). It's much easier than you might think. Simply put, clean food is naturally grown and minimally processed. In the opening thirty-five pages, Terry offers a primer on clean eating and includes not only a list of ways to improve health and well-being (#1 chew,

---

chew, chew) but an entire section on "Basic Cooking Methods" that will make a life-time of cooking whole foods a snap.

She puts her preaching into practice with 223 delicious and seasonal recipes that are quick to make and chock-full of nutrients. From spring's bright *Swiss Chard with Roasted Golden Beets and Sweet Peas,* right on through to winter's *Spicy Coconut and Pumpkin Soup,* Terry's food surprises and satisfies. She makes cleaning up your diet—and body—seem easy and fun.

Terry is not a boring, proselytizing, overearnest vegan. Cooking teacher, marathon runner, wife, and mother of two, she's just the kind of woman who can show your readers and viewers how to make easy and positive changes in their diet (and lifestyle) that will make a difference—for them and the earth. And yes, we promise, your kids will eat it.

I am enclosing an advance copy for your review. We'll be in touch soon to discuss scheduling an interview with Terry. Please let us know if you have any questions.

Best,
Kimberly Yorio and Aimee Bianca
kim@ycmedia.com and *aimee@ycmedia.com*

New-Business Proposals

You write proposals to win new business. For a current client, it can be as simple as a two-paragraph e-mail outlining your scope of work and fee. For a potential client, it can be as complex as a two-hundred-page response to a formal "Request for Proposal" (RFP) for a technical project. Whatever the size, all proposals are selling documents—an attempt to convince the potential client that you are the most qualified and best-suited to do the work.

When major corporations, government agencies, and large nonprofit organizations undertake significant projects or large purchases they release RFPs. RFPs are extremely specific and generally mammoth documents. They clearly spell out everything the buyer wants to see from your company as well as how they want you to deliver the material. They also include deadlines. And none of the contents is negotiable. You must respond exactly as requested.

When you are considering responding to this kind of proposal, be certain you pass the minimum requirements. These formal proposals are incredibly time-consuming (actually, all proposals are). You have to use the resources of your marketing, technical, and financial teams to put them together. Imagine the drain on company resources if you were continually responding to proposals you couldn't ever qualify for. If you find you are too small to respond to most of the big jobs out there, consider teaming up with a larger operation and becoming a subcontractor for them.

If you choose not to bid, always send a TBNT letter, "Thanks But No Thanks." Thank them for the opportunity and tell them that you aren't the right fit for this RFP but to please consider you for their next project.

If you are putting together a proposal without an RFP, deciding what to include can be challenging. Each proposal should be developed from scratch, because boilerplates can generally be sniffed out a mile away. You should have a consistent format and style for your proposals, but the content should be original—except for the sections that describe company capabilities or biographies. What follows are the components that you should include and/or consider.

Goal(s) or Objective(s): Clearly outline the goals or objectives for the project. Interview your prospective client thoroughly and make sure you understand what that person or collection of people wants, and create a program that addresses those needs.

Marketplace Assessment: Show your client that you understand her business and the opportunities and challenges that are facing her.

Strategies: Write a detailed plan that shows how you plan to capitalize on the opportunities and overcome the challenges of the client's business. For example, if one of the challenges is that budgets are small (which is probably the most common challenge), you can include a list of low-cost strategies. However, we caution you not to be too detailed. The genius in a proposal is to be clear yet vague enough that if you don't get the business, the client won't be able to use your proposal as a manual. Remember if a client requests a proposal and you submit one, they own it—whether you get the business or not.

Capabilities: Drop in the description of your company's capabilities, and move on to the next part. This is the only spot appropriate for boilerplate material.

Cost and Timeline: Outline your fees and the timeline you forecast to accomplish your goals.

Appendices: Include any third-party source material that confirms your capabilities. In our business we include copies of media clips that we generate, but you could include a detailed client list or a list of references.

WE LEARNED THE HARD WAY

We got the chance to submit a proposal to a very large company. We were going up against three other firms, all of which were triple our size and had triple our billing. We thought the only way to win the business would be to really show our stuff in the proposal. We dropped all of our current work (and one of us even suspended her vacation) to do a kick-ass job on it. We hired our freelance graphic designer to make the material look interesting and had it printed and bound. It was a work of art—great looking and full of great strategies, painstakingly outlined in detail. We didn't get the business—because we were too small. The company liked us so much that the winning agency has contracted us to do portions of the program. And guess what we found out? The winning firm is actually implementing our program. Now, we can't be sure they didn't come up with the same ideas, but, boy, it feels really familiar.

We learned a few other lessons in this process:

If you are lucky, one person will actually read the entire proposal cover to cover. The rest just kind of skim it while they are listening to your presentation.

Don't overload it with details. We spent endless hours putting together specific lists and budgets, trying to wow them with our competence. It didn't make a difference. They were looking for a bigger agency.

Don't believe everything you hear. We really were misled in this process. Our client contact was presenting herself as the key decision maker when she was merely one piece of the management team (and actually the lowest-ranking member). She led us to believe that she would advocate for us even though we were uncomfortably small for the company. She also gave us poor advice about what her management team was looking for in strategy. Generally, the higher-ups want to see big-picture strategy and hear plenty of examples of how you've executed similar campaigns for other folks.

POWERLESS WITH POWERPOINT: HOW TO GET GOING WITH THIS PRESENTATION PROGRAM

Sarilee Norton has been an executive in the packaging industry for more than thirty years, specializing in management and strategic planning. She's created hundreds of presentations throughout her corporate career and made them the foundation of her consulting practice with Dock Sqaure Consultants. She tells us that "in the old days" (the mid-1990s), presentations were done using 35-millimeter slides created at a slide house. Each slide typically cost between $50 and $100. They were expensive and inflexible. In order to change them, a brand-new slide had to be created. Budgets and common sense forced her to investigate other options—and she found PowerPoint. What follows is Sarilee's primer on writing effective and memorable PowerPoint presentations.

- Identify key messages. Begin by identifying the five or six messages you want your audience to take away. A good rule of thumb is to allow sixty seconds per slide. If you are creating a twenty-minute presentation, don't have many more than twenty foundation slides. (Some points make take five slides to explain.)

- Write your script and presentation at the same time. Use the "notes" feature to make it easier. Generally, if you are presenting to a large formal audience, write a very detailed script that includes cues for changing the slide.

- Presentations aren't meant to be read word for word. The beauty of the program is that it offers a zillion tools so that you can visually demonstrate your message. Use PowerPoint to pace the presentation and project the things that you want your audience to be thinking about while you are talking.

- When you present to a small group and can maintain eye contact and read body language, forgo the screen and do the presentation from hard copies.

- If you use bulleted text, limit the number of words. Do not put up paragraphs. The points should be simple and easy to read. When you put too many words up on screen, the typeface gets too small for the audience to read and makes it a struggle to pay attention to your presentation.

- Use other visuals as part of the slides—clip art, photographs, charts or illustrations, animations, or video. At least every fourth slide should have a visual element.

- Use small sounds or music to get people's attention, but use it sparingly. Too many sound effects could overwhelm a presentation.

- Be careful about color selections. Primary colors work better for simple charts. Certain colors create vibration. Go to the back of the room where you are delivering the presentation and make sure it is pleasing to the eye. Avoid a white background because they make letters vibrate. If you need a light background, then choose beige or gray.

- Distribute handouts whenever possible—especially if the presentation contains technical or scientific data.

- Avoid too many bells and whistles. PowerPoint is so easy that new users tend to go crazy. They create a bar graph simply because they can.

A note about contracts: Don't make a big deal when you sign the deal

Contracts should be a very simple agreement between two parties outlining the terms of their arrangement. You should create a standard version for your company that you get vetted by your attorney and then fill in the blanks from there. In most cases, you should avoid legalese (unless, of course, your business is the law) and use plain language.

the word	**Rebecca Ryan, Founder**
	Next Generation Consulting

When we interviewed Rebecca, we were extremely impressed by her smarts and chutzpah. She's a trained economist who started her consulting business after a near-death experience snowshoeing in the backcountry of Wisconsin. While hopelessly lost in the woods, she decided there was no way she was going to her grave working for somebody else. The next day she quit her job and called everybody she knew and told them that she was an expert. She began lecturing and collecting data. Along the way she picked up clients, added staff, and generally created a fantastically successful and interesting company. She did some brilliant things, like hiring a service to answer her phones during business hours and getting a small bank loan to fund her growth. But what really blew us away was her use of jargon, buzzwords, and acronyms. There really is a whole different world out there, and the people in it are communicating in some pretty strange ways. We chose to share several of her quotes.

- Young people need to figure out if they are a careerist or a change-artist.

- Our mission and vision statement point to our true north. We went around a table and asked where everybody's juice came from and created: "Mission: To build next-generation companies and community; and Vision: Our next generation will live and work in stimulating and humane environments."

- I have this very simple exercise that I call ACE: What will I ADD to what I am currently doing to make me more successful? What will I CHANGE that I currently do to make me more successful? What will I ELIMINATE to make me more successful?

- One of the coolest things about our company is that we are a completely virtual company with a one hundred percent distributed workforce. Next Generation Consulting is a research think tank devoted to researching and reporting on Generation X's living and working trends.

- We are hired by companies in the financial services, insurance, and legal sectors looking down their time-horizon and worried about future staffing. We've also expanded recently into the community-service space. For example, the state of Iowa is desperate to attract younger people to their state. We do quantifiable and qualitative analysis to create "community handprints" that demonstrate the "coolness" of their state.

- What I hear in my research is that their [business-women's] older male counterparts treat them like their wives or daughters. And I think that this will end with the baby boomers. I myself have not run into any gender bias. I've been fortunate in that I've had male advocates. The reality of the industries that I work in—banking, legal, and insurance—is that you need what I like to call, "PMS buy-in." If you get pale, male, and stale on board, then you have no problem.

- Next Generation defines X'ers as the four Ss: skeptical of institution, savvy with technology and information, self-reliant, and speedy.

TEN PROOFREADING PITFALLS
FROM A MASTER WORDSMITH

Judith Sutton is a copy editor, editor, and consultant for cookbooks. She has worked on more than 250 books and won't even begin to project the number of manuscript pages that have crossed her desk. She guest lectures at New York University about copyediting and offers her most-noticed proofreading pitfalls and tips for avoiding them.

1. Don't trust spell-check. I turned mine off the day I bought my computer. You might have the wrong word in the wrong place, but if it's spelled correctly, it won't register as an error.

2. Even people who know better are afraid to use "me." They will write, "He called Tom and I" instead of the grammatically correct, "He called Tom and me." "Me" is not a bad word; use it when the objective case is appropriate.

3. Some common definitions: "Disinterested" does not mean "not interested." It means "impartial." "Hard" is a state of being, the

opposite of "soft." "Difficult" means "hard to do." "Discreet" means "on the down low." "Discrete" means "separate."

4. The "it's," "its" thing. "It is" and "its," the possessive pronoun, are completely different animals. Read your sentence aloud and if "it's" can be replaced with "it is," then make sure you include the apostrophe.

5. Dangling modifiers: "Made with a variety of wonderful Mediterranean fish and shellfish, I love bouillabaisse." (I don't think the writer intended to describe herself as "wonderful Mediterranean fish and shellfish.") This sentence should read: "I love bouillabaisse, which is made with a variety of wonderful Mediterranean fish and shellfish."

6. Avoid jargon and business-speak. Aim for a professional but somewhat conversational style, depending on your audience, of course.

7. Avoid the other extreme and don't be overly casual.

8. Avoid wordiness and repetition. You can often, without realizing it, use the same word twice in the same sentence or three times in the same paragraph.

9. Read your writing out loud. At the very least, you will be able to identify if you sound normal.

10. It's *much* easier to catch mistakes when you print out your writing and then read it rather than when you read it on a computer screen. Print front and back if you want to save paper.

If you are unsure about your grammar and writing skills, keep copies nearby of Patricia T. O'Conner's *Woe Is I: The Grammarphobe's Guide to Better English in Plain English* and Bryson's *Dictionary of Troublesome Words: A Writer's Guide to Getting It Right.*

And if you truly can't write to save your life, it's worth outsourcing or bartering with someone who can. Just remember that you are ultimately responsible for everything that goes out under your name.

| **Sara Kate Gillingham-Ryan, Editor and Blogger**

Sara Kate Gillingham-Ryan, a food writer based in New York City, is also the founding editor of Apartment Therapy's The Kitchn (*www.thekitchn.com*), an award-winning cooking blog covering recipes, product and book reviews, tips, and inspiration. To be honest, when we first met Sara Kate, we didn't give enough respect to blogs, which have now become a daily part of life (especially in our PR lives). But we have the utmost respect for S.K., who has been able to parlay a successful, profitable, full-time business from what started as a side project. A pioneer of food blogs, The Kitchn is one of several sites under the Apartment Therapy Media umbrella, a network of blogs with more than 4 million unique visitors per month, started with her husband, Maxwell Gillingham-Ryan.

In addition to her on-line work, Sara Kate writes the monthly cookbook column for *House Beautiful* magazine and is at work on a book about cooking for a crowd. She has written nationally syndicated food articles for Tribune Media and done writing and recipe development work for *Food & Wine*, *Oprah Magazine*, *Bon Appétit*, and *Muscle & Fitness*. She is also the author of *The Greyston Bakery Cookbook: More Than 80 Recipes to Inspire the Way You Cook and Live* (Rodale, 2007). We spoke to Sara Kate about the early days of her blog and how she became one of the first profitable (and most respected) food sites on-line.

Tell us about the process for launching Apartment Therapy and The Kitchn: You did this together, right?

Apartment Therapy was started as a design practice by my husband in 2001 after we both witnessed the World Trade Center collapse from the corner of Broadway and Spring Street. Time for a life change. He was an elementary school teacher with a design background. I was in the nonprofit world and itching to go to culinary school and become a food writer. His design practice evolved into a web site in 2004 after he started sending out weekly e-mails on an interior-design-related topic ("Apartment Therapy on Spring Cleaning," "Apartment Therapy on Getting Rid of Your Record Collection," "Apartment Therapy on Hanging Curtains," etc.) and his brother, hailing from Silicon Valley, said we should make a blog out of it instead of "throwing away the content"—true! So we did. In addition to my freelance writing, I was writing food pieces once a week; I think it was a column called "Nourishment" (back when we titled all the columns). One day it occurred to us that people who are into their home are for the most part into cooking as well, which led to a separate site. At that point we'd only spun off other cities (I think we had Los Angeles and had launched San Francisco around the same time as The Kitchn, late 2005.) So we're coming up on six years for the web sites and five for The Kitchn.

Can you tell us about the design process for the site? How has it evolved? How has the programming evolved?
Originally, it was on TypePad, one of several amateur, user-friendly blogging programs available for a few bucks a month. We pretty quickly turned to Moveable Type (their customizable version for professionals) and had a friend—a great designer named Brenda Rotheiser (www.wink-design.com), who is the creative director for Vosges Haut-Chocolat—help us.

The programming evolved from friend helping to the big leap—an expensive part-time guy who worked for Gawker. We then hired that guy more regularly, and finally, we moved on to what we have now: a full-time in-house programmer. We need another, but it's a big leap again. We're waiting for the right moment. Sometime in 2010, I imagine.

When did you realize it was a viable business?
We started thinking we could do this and live off of it a few years ago, and Max stopped seeing design clients in 2007. But we didn't make a profit until 2009.

Biggest challenges? Biggest rewards?
The biggest challenge in running a business is that for a long time we've had to do everything ourselves, and that includes things that are not our strengths. When you're hired for a job it's usually because you're good at something: whether it's a receptionist position and you have a good voice and are organized or it's a programmer job and you know tech and don't mind staring at screens all day. With starting this on our own, we've had to do a lot that we're not good at. A lot of baptism by fire. Management isn't easy and neither of us have ever wanted to be bosses. Max is getting better at it though. He's pretty amazing to watch.

The biggest rewards are knowing we help people (the sites now reach more than 4 million unique visitors each month), providing jobs (thirteen full-time and about seventy part-time writers), and getting to create something every single day. Now that I'm a mother, it feels very rewarding that we get to raise our child in an environment where she sees her parents striving all the time and making exciting things that help people. That's what on-line media is to us: an opportunity to make something that helps people. As a cook, I really get that. There is a lot of crossover between cooking and making an on-line publication. Odd, but true.

Knowing what you know now, what would you have done differently in the beginning?
Sprung for a few more massages and made a strict rule about when the computer gets shut off. We don't own a television and are vehement about not having it in our lives, yet the computers

are on constantly. When you run your own business, the boundaries get fuzzy. And you forget to manage your stress—hence the massages.

I'd also like to suggest these resources:

> *Writer's Market* (also available on-line for about $30 per year at *www.writersmarket.com*)
>
> *The Elements of Style*, by William Strunk and E. B. White
>
> ProfNet (*www.profnet.com*); this free service helps journalists find people to interview for articles

10

It Couldn't Hurt:
Good Business Advice Your Grandmother Would Have Given You (and Maybe Did)

Our grandmothers were smart women who had a great deal to say about how we should live our lives. We are sure that, had they had the opportunities that exist today, our grandmothers would have also issued some great business advice along with their admonishments to *never go to bed angry* and *never leave the house without lipstick on*. This chapter will offer some very grandmotherly advice, including how to make your business a success, find a mentor, reenergize yourself, and work with a partner. All that, plus a lot of encouragement.

Five Rules for Making Your Business a Success

1. **YOU DEFINE SUCCESS.** If you started your business so you could have more time for your kids and you now make it to their school plays, your business is a success.

2. **LISTEN TO YOUR INSTINCTS, WHETHER YOU LIKE THE ANSWER OR NOT.** If you get a bad feeling about anything, listen to it.

3. **DO RESEARCH, RESEARCH, AND MORE RESEARCH.** You are going to be making some very big decisions during the course of

your business ownership. Before you jump in and make decisions that could have negative consequences, do your research.

4. **LOVE TO LEARN.** Since you will be learning about new things all the time, every day, you want to embrace the process.

5. **KNOW WHAT YOU ARE GETTING INTO.** All of the women we spoke to advised that before deciding to launch a business, you know what you are getting into. If you have prepared yourself for the commitment, it will make the time that you devote to it that much more enjoyable.

Suck Up: Sending Cards, Notes, and Gifts

As a business owner you will need to think about how to thank, recognize, show appreciation for, congratulate, and woo those in your professional circle, or those you want to be, in a way that is unique to you and your business. Think about those generic holiday cards you get from your doctor's office each year. You may appreciate the effort, but it feels a bit impersonal, doesn't it? To personalize the thought, you might want to enlist the designer who created your corporate identity to make thank-you cards, gift boxes, or notepaper in your style. Beyond that, we have outlined below a few times when a little something extra is a good business move.

The Big Thank-you

We are big advocates of the thank-you note or gift, depending on the kindness. If someone gives you a referral, send a thank-you note. If the referral turns into business, then send a gift. If someone gives you advice, send a thank-you note. If someone goes out of their way for you, send a thank-you note. And when we say "note," we mean handwritten on notepaper. Avoid e-mailing a thank-you; we know you are busy, but it looks lazy. People will remember when you don't thank them. Two years ago we sent a former employer a referral that turned out to be a big project for her agency. She never called us to thank us for the business, and we felt unappreciated. People feel good about your business when you recognize them in some way and will remember it when they're not.

Happy Holidays

Send holiday cards, especially in the first year, to everyone you have done business with. If you have core clients who contributed to making your business a success, then a holiday gift is in order. Take some time to choose an appropriate gift; don't wait until the last minute. One of our former employers sent cards to most everyone, and for those special clients, who spent lots of money on hiring her, she handpicked very expensive, personal gifts. We have our holiday cards designed—since we are in the food business, we add a holiday recipe—and send them to everyone in our database. For our clients, we find a boutique food shop that can create unique gift baskets for us, and then we work with them to handpick the items. The point is to personalize the holiday greeting, because you want the person receiving the card or gift to be happy to get it and happier that you were the one who sent it.

Birthdays

For certain businesses, it is beneficial to know the birthdays of your customers or clients. If you open a restaurant in a small town and you have some locals who consistently dine there, learn and remember everyone's birthday. That way you can send over a slice of cake or a sundae with a candle in it as your way of saying "happy birthday" and "thank you for being my customer." Even restaurants in big cities have started to computerize their reservation system, and many will ask what your birthday is so that they will be aware of it when the time comes.

At the very least, if you learn that it is the birthday of one of your customers when they are in your establishment, send over a glass of wine if you run a restaurant, give a discount if you run a boutique, or offer a bouquet if you run a flower shop. It will be appreciated and not soon forgotten, and better yet, the story of the gift will be shared with everyone your customer knows.

Bridal and Baby Showers

Some business owners would benefit from taking the time to acknowledge the weddings and baby showers of their customers. If you open a hair salon and you hear that your client is getting married, send a congratulations note, because maybe she will be looking for someone to do the hair of everyone in the wedding party. If you launch a children's clothing store and a customer tells you that she is expecting another child, send a gift. It will help build loyalty and soon you will have another customer.

Congratulations!

If you hear that an important customer has gotten some great news (new job, engagement, she is expecting), send a note or a bouquet as a congratulations. Again, it is a goodwill gesture that will pay off down the line.

Finding a Mentor: Do You Have Some Advice?

A mentor is someone who "has been there, done that" and is willing to share what she has learned with you. A mentor is someone who can give you sound, objective advice that actually makes sense. Do not mistake a friendly competitor who has some suggestions for your business for a mentor. Do not look to a wise person who has no knowledge of your business to be your mentor. A mentor is hard to find, and when you do, thank your lucky stars. "I define a healthy relationship with a mentor as one that is mutually beneficial. I look to my mentor for advice and guidance, and in return, I am there for her, offering the same thing," says Tara Paterson founder of *www.justformom.com*, a web community for moms.

There is an element of luck (or fate, for those who believe in the notion) to finding a mentor, but we have some suggestions for where to start looking.

A great place to start is the Office of Women's Business Ownership, at *www.sba.gov/womeninbusiness/wnet.html* (part of the Small Business Association). They oversee a huge network of women's business centers. Or try a local chapter of a women's business organization, such as the National Association of Women Business Owners or your local chamber of commerce. They frequently offer workshops, lunches, and lectures, where you can interact with many potential mentors.

If you have a community college or university in your area, do some digging; maybe the dean of the business school is a generous and knowledgeable soul who likes nothing more than to give advice to female entrepreneurs.

Join a local chapter of a professional organization for your industry. Many of the women you will meet may be competitors, but then again luck may be with you.

Too Much Information: Keeping Your Emotions at Home

No one said it would be easy. No one said that there were not going to be frustrating days, brewing arguments, crippling tension, and out-of-control anxiety. But when you run your own business, it is more important than ever to KEEP YOUR EMOTIONS AT HOME! It is very hard to do, because all you need is one sympathetic employee to catch you after a bad phone call to challenge your resolve to *keep it to yourself*. The ramifications, though, for sharing your emotions with that employee are significant. Maybe she interprets your frustration as instability and shares her new "the-boss-is-crazy" theory with her coworkers, and suddenly the dynamic in your office has changed.

Let's be honest. Women tend to be more emotional about business matters (actually about life in general) than men, and this has given us a bad rap. We need to transcend the stereotype of the "hysterical" female business owner and handle confrontations, uncomfortable conversations with customers, complaints, employee reviews, etc., without the emotion. Try to take out the emotional language when you are talking about business. Words like *feel*, *hurt*, and *disappointed* have no place in the workplace. Trust us on this one.

Keeping emotions at home does not mean that you shouldn't express your frustration at an employee or a difficult client. We are just saying not to put it in emotional terms. "The fact that you misspelled that customer's name pissed me off" and "Any loser could tell that shirt wasn't on sale" wouldn't be the way to go. "You need to make your note-taking skills a priority" and "I am sorry that it wasn't clearer, but that shirt is not on sale," would be better.

Partners as Friends

Partners are a mixed blessing when it comes to this no-emotion-in-the-workplace challenge. They are fantastic when you need to vent; they are a godsend after a bad phone call with a significant other; they are always on your side (or should be) when a customer has given you a hard time. But the negatives of turning to your partner for this kind of emotional support are numerous.

You don't want to establish a pattern of taking up the workday discussing personal issues.

You don't want to get used to talking about business as an emotional element in your life. Sure, it is at the core, but it will be difficult to deal with all of the other people in your professional circle who believe that"business is business" if you continue to think of it emotionally.

If you start depending on your partner as your ear, it will make it difficult for you when you are dealing with tension between you. If your partner has spent the last month hearing about your breakup, how comfortable are you going to be bringing up her poor sales figures? Not very.

It is easy for negativity to feed off negativity. If you spend time each day griping about customers, your landlord, the printer, bills, or your employees with your partner, it will start to bring you both down.

Employees as Friends

Worse than expressing emotions to your partner is sharing them with your employees. That is a big fat NO. For starters, you don't want (nor do you have time to hear) their problems, so don't bother them with yours, because it will set a precedent. Additionally, you don't want to encourage your employees to think of work as a place where emotions belong. They don't. Keep it professional with your employees, and they will keep it professional with you and your customers. The way it should be.

Customers as Friends

You share your problems with friends or therapists but not with your customers. If they share, that is fine—it will help build loyalty and perhaps even a real friendship down the line. But keep your emotional life to yourself. If you don't, you might have customers doubting your level of service or talking to their friends about their doubts about the longevity of your business or your difficulties with your vendors. The only talking you want people to do about you is praising your products or services (or at the very least, your new haircut).

TEN TIPS FOR REENERGIZING YOURSELF

1. Take a moment to relive the days of working for someone else. For some, that flashback of an old boss reprimanding them is enough to make them feel really thankful that they are now running their own business.

2. Pilates, yoga, meditation, prayer. Every woman we interviewed for this book took a little time each day to focus on her spiritual well-being. This can contribute to your general feeling of happiness as well as being a great stress-buster.

3. If you are feeling really low and unenthusiastic about your business, leave it for a few minutes, an hour, or an afternoon. Go outside, walk around, take a drive, or go to a chick flick. What your mind and body are telling you is that you need a break.

4. Review everything you have learned about yourself since you launched your business. You will be amazed at how much you have changed and grown since starting this adventure.

5. Review everything you have learned about business since you started your own. We mean everything from taxes to hiring and firing someone. You now understand so much more about the world of business than most people. Even the most brilliant MBA working for a financial firm has less hands-on business experience than you do.

6. You might be bored. Expand your professional circle. Start writing an article for a business publication, join a women's business organization, or do some pro bono work for an organization you believe in.

7. Take a class. It doesn't have to be business-related. Sometimes all you need to get reenergized is to do something for yourself; stimulating your brain is a great way to go. If you don't have the time to take a class during the day, check out on-line options. We just recently finished an on-line writing course through the Gotham Writers' Workshop, and we had the flexibility of doing the homework assignments when we could get around to it.

8. Pick up a hobby. You might just be tired of spending your focus on one thing all the time. If you read, join or start a book club. If you have always wanted to learn how to knit, do it. If you like to hike, join a hiking club. Whatever it may be, it will make you a more rounded and more interesting person if you follow your personal as well as professional bliss.

9. **See your friends.** Spending time with them is a great way to be reenergized about your life. Spending social time with friends is always healthy and not talking about business even better. And we know this sounds selfish, after hearing about how much your friend hates her boss, you might really appreciate what you have going.

10. **Add new services.** You may be ready to expand your business. The challenge of launching a new service can give you a boost in energy, and hopefully, profits.

"Read the Newspaper Every Day"

Over the years we have had some very wise people impart some very wise advice to us about running a business. Tara Paterson said her mother taught her that "I could accomplish anything if I put my mind to it; there are no barriers." In addition to that supportive and sage advice, we wanted to share some other words of wisdom with you. Don't consider the source, because you don't know any of these people (unless you know our mothers, Sharyn Yorio or Joan Bredin-Price), but do think about this advice and try it out. Soon you will realize how sound it really is.

"You should know a little bit about everything, because when you do, you will always have something to talk about with everyone you meet."

We encourage you to follow this advice because it has proved incredibly helpful for us. Because we are in public relations, the chances that we will be seated next to a stranger at a multihour event are pretty good; so being able to talk a little bit about movies, restaurants, sports, travel, politics, and religion (although we avoid the last two topics if possible) has been a lifesaver. But even if you open a pet-grooming shop, your customers are essentially strangers, so it is great to have at your disposal a variety of topics you are comfortable discussing. It will help you feel confident when you go into a group of strangers and adds to the comfort level of your customers and clients.

"Read the newspaper every day."

In addition to the fact that you should always be up-to-date about what is happening locally and nationally, you should read the paper every day because you never know when something related to your business will appear in the paper. Maybe it will be that a potential new location is for sale; one of your customers was elected as a town official; a competitor is moving in; or a competitor is closing shop. The world is a constantly changing place, and no matter what your business is, you should be tracking opportunities and challenges. The easiest way to do this is by reading the newspaper in whatever form suits you.

"Pick a profession that will happily and comfortably merge with your personal life."

We had a former employer who invited her staff to her weekend house for yearly retreats, had dinner with her clients, and threw holiday parties for her vendors and potential clients. When we asked why she did this, she said, "because I picked a business I love so much that I make it an extension of my personal life." Okay, so maybe we don't want to go as far as inviting our web designer to join our book club, but we have made friends out of clients and made lunches with potential new customers fun rather than work. We do agree that the business should complement your personal life, because if it doesn't, it isn't the right fit for you.

"Vacations help your business."

There was a two-year period when we didn't take vacations. Did this help our business? NO. Entrepreneurs need vacations as much, if not more, than those who work for other people. You have a lot on your shoulders as a business owner, and without some downtime, you will burn out, and that doesn't help your business. Burnout can manifest itself in a grouchy disposition, lack of creativity, low energy, and depression. But if you force yourself to take some time off (on the beach with an iPhone and laptop doesn't count), you will find yourself reinspired and reenergized, and you will return to work feeling recommitted to making your business a success.

"Do what you say you are going to do."

That means that if you tell a customer you are going to research a product for them, do it. If you tell your landlord you will move crates away from the fire door, do it. You told an employee you will give them a review in a month, you better schedule it. Why? Because really, all you have is your word and your reputation, and to keep both intact—do what you say you are going to do. You want to be someone who people can rely on.

"Sometimes it is better to be a mensch."

This is a tough one because being a mensch is not always in your best interest as a business owner. But in the long run, it will make you feel better about yourself as a human being and will make others feel better about you. Being a mensch does not mean being a sucker. It means taking the high road knowing it would have been easier and cheaper to take the low. You have hired a freelancer this week to help you with shipping five hundred cases of chocolate. The manufacturer just called and they are going to run two days late with the delivery. You know the freelancer has counted on the money for those two days. Be a mensch and give her other work to do if you have it. It won't cost you that much money, and the freelancer will work *very* hard for you. A customer returns a book to your bookstore. She has come in two weeks past the deadline for a cash-back return, but that is what she wants. Be a mensch and give her the refund. It just isn't worth fighting over, and it would make her feel better about you and your store if you refunded her the money.

Compromise and Caring
(Working with a Partner)

Chef Jody Adams, from the Rialto restaurant, calls a partnership a "marriage." And in many ways it is. Like in a marriage, with a partnership you have another person 50 percent invested in the relationship, money, and operations of your business. This is a very intimate relationship that needs constant reevaluation. As with a spouse, you can never take your partnership for granted. And you need to be honest about what you need from the partnership and what you can give to the partnership. You also need to listen to what your partner needs from the partnership.

This type of business relationship is challenging, but when it is a good one, it affords you a fantastic opportunity to grow both professionally and personally. If you pick the right partner, that person complements your strengths and the business is that much stronger. If you pick the right partner, she can help the business be a fun and inspirational place to be. If the partnership is healthy, you can broach difficult issues, like the value of what each of you is contributing to the business or the differences you have with management style, without an argument.

Respect Your Partner

Especially during difficult times, remember why you decided on this person to partner with. The reason was probably (and should be) that you respect her work ethic and talent. Respect your partner's point of view, because although you may disagree with it you need to acknowledge your partner's right to have it.

Respect Your Partnership

Take a little bit of time each week or month to discuss with your partner whether the structure of the business is still working for both of you. You may be surprised to hear that she wants to change her schedule because she has decided to take a class or that she is frustrated with the amount of time she is spending on tax issues with the accountant. Whatever it is or isn't, you both need to be content with the structure of the business, and the only way to gauge that is by checking in with each other.

Talk About the Business

Not the partnership but the nitty-gritty of the business. We tend to talk about the small business issues that arise almost daily, and we schedule time once a month to talk about the bigger issues. There needs to be an ongoing dialogue about the business. When you do have these meetings or catch-ups, treat them as you would any other meeting. If you come into it with an agenda listing out the items for discussion, you will find the meeting much more productive and you won't slip into talking about the outfits the new secretary has been sporting since she joined Weight Watchers. Take these meetings seriously, and we say that because it is much easier to just have fun.

Keep Your Ego Out of It

This is very hard for some people. But when you work with another person, you really need to try to not make everything about you. Decisions should be made with the best interest of the company in mind (and if you need a third party to give objective feedback, get a mediator), and you should not personalize the discussion or disagreement. The only bumps that we encounter occur when one of us has allowed our ego to get in the way of a decision.

Keeping the Family Happy
(And More Important, Happy for You)

Tara Paterson was raised by a mother who "never let me forget that I was number one with her." Making sure your family feels that same way when you are trying to juggle a demanding business is not easy, but the solution for Tara and other entrepreneurs is to maintain harmony. Not just within one's self but for the whole family.

Every entrepreneur should dedicate time and focus on every family member every day. Give time and energy to yourself first, so that you are not depleted (easier said than done, but a fifteen-minute meditation or yoga stretch can really help); make sure that your children have private time with you; spend time on your business; and of course don't forget your significant other. When everyone is "filled," as Tara puts it, they will support you and your business without resentment.

We interieved hundreds of women for our book *Happy at Work, Happy at Home: The Girl's Guide to Being a Working Mom*, and were reminded again and again to pay attention to one's significant other. Your romantic partner has been with you through some tough times, and there will be more down the road. So show that you appreciate the support and caring by spending some time with this person. Your romantic partner can be a source of strength for you if you take some time to nurture the relationship.

| the word | **Joan Saperstan,** **Licensed Independent Clinical Social Worker** |

When you start a new business, it is almost a little like falling in love. You are excited about spending time on the business; maybe you want to spend more time working. It is natural for your personal relationships to slip a little during the beginning stages of entrepreneurship. What you don't want is for this to continue, because you don't want your significant other or your children to start resenting your business.

If you are sensing that your family is beginning to resent the time and energy you are spending on the business and are increasingly angry at you for not being there for them, you need to take a close look at how you are relating to them.

It is a quantity issue, when you are just not taking enough time out of the day to be with your family. If that is the case, you may need to reduce your hours or take on more help at the workplace.

Or it may be a quality issue, and you need to be actively participating in the family—listening, asking questions, joining activities.

When Business Is Slow
(And It Can Be Slow Sometimes)

Nancy Forman, of Language Liaison, says, "Slow times allow me to pull back and do things I usually don't have the time to do." Many people pull back on spending and do more of the work themselves, which is a really great way to get back to the nuts and bolts of your business. There is nothing like filing paperwork, answering phones, and paying bills yourself to get you back in touch with the basics of how your business runs.

Sherry Treco-Jones, president of Treco-Jones Public Relations, recommends that during slow times you "continue to market—focus on new business and building existing business, and stay visible. Use the downtime to review and revise business processes as needed, and catch up on administrative tasks. This could include changing your billing policies for projects to include advance payments. In the event of more extreme economic issues, watch your numbers—that is, revise income projections, and review and realign your budget. You do not want your spending to exceed revenues. Do not 'count your chickens before they hatch': i.e., do not include your prospects' revenues in your budgeting until a contract is signed."

Elaine Haber says that when her accounting business is slow, she tries to gauge how long it is going to remain slow. If she has a client that is only taking a break from her services, then she might take the time to take a class to help hone her skills. If it is for a longer period of time, she will make calls to try to get another client to fill the void.

We recommend that you examine the factors that are contributing to your business slowing down. Is your business seasonal? If it is busy only in the winter months, you may want to consider changing your business or expanding your services a bit so they appeal to customers in the warmer months. Is it the economy? If so, there is little you can do about that but buckle down, spend less money, and wait it out. If your competitors are still doing well and have not experienced a dip in business, you need to reexamine your business to see what isn't working. It is a good idea to talk to your bookkeeper and accountant at this time to see if you are spending your money wisely.

Failure: How Do You Know It Is Coming?
(And How to Deal with It When It Does)

The reality is that some businesses fail. The reasons for failure can be as varied as a poor business plan to it was just the wrong economic market and time to launch. As a business owner, you will know that failure is coming if you pay attention to your finances outlined in your profit-and-loss statements. If you are consistently losing money, your customers are dwindling away, and there is no chance that things are going to turn around quickly enough for you to pay your bills, then your business is failing. We are not talking about a dip; we are talking about a consistent downward trend in your income and prospects. At this point, take control of what is happening and talk to your accountant and lawyer. They can see what is happening and give you a realistic projection for how long you can stay afloat.

A business failure is a scary thing to go through. But as Jody Adams told us after her Red Clay restaurant failed, "I learned more about the process of launching a restaurant when I did one that didn't work." For those who are now on the other side of a failure, like Jody, they see the experience as an opportunity to reprioritize. She advises that after a failure you "move on, see it as a learning process, and know that you need to be more careful with taking on projects in the future."

Ten Mantras to Get You Through the Day

There are some sentences that women business owners end up frequently saying to themselves to help them through the challenges that come up as an entrepreneur. These are a few that have helped us and also helped the women we spoke to.

1. Competition is healthy
As a woman it is hard to accept that you are competitive without a little bit of shame. We encourage you to embrace this aspect of yourself, because it will contribute to your success.

2. I can do this
You can confront a landlord, sign a new account, and take out a loan for an office renovation. None of it will kill you, so why be scared? Go into each situation knowing you can do it.

3. I deserve this
For all of the women we spoke to, this was the hardest emotional state to reach. Most of us, even if we are at the top of our game, question whether we are worthy. To counter that, we suggest that you start each

day saying this to yourself. Corny, yes, but believe us, it will make you feel good.

4. Sometimes I *am* right

When dealing with a difficult customer or a problematic vendor, it is easy to buckle. Sometimes you have to just for the sake of the business, but sometimes you are right and you need to get over your insecurities and take a stand. So tell yourself, "Yes, I am right!"

5. It is my business

You need to own your business on every level. If a contractor did something incorrectly, you point it out and make them redo it. Why? Because it is your business.

6. It's not personal; it is just business

This is a great mantra to have on hand for all of those really tough situations, such as firing an employee. It is necessary to emotionally step back from your business sometimes, and this can help.

7. I belong

Sometimes when you are attending a chamber of commerce meeting or a professional conference or speaking on a panel, you may feel out of place. You may question your participation. Don't. You belong.

8. It is okay to be wrong

For some, apologizing is physically painful, but when you own your business, you will occasionally be wrong about something. You ordered the wrong thing for a customer, the steak your chef made was overcooked, or you overcharged a client. Admitting you were wrong not only is the best tack to take for business but is the right thing to do.

9. There are some things that are out of my control

You fulfill a client's order by mail and it gets lost; the manufacturer that sews your handbags sent you the right bags in the wrong fabric; your phones go out because of a storm. There are a million things that you can control about your business. And some you can't. It is better to make peace with that on a daily basis, because you don't know what could go wrong today.

10. I am proud of myself

Your business is finally making a profit; you were just written up in the local paper; or you have enough money to hire another employee. You feel good, right? That feeling is pride. And sometimes, it is good and right to feel pride. Not everyone has it in them to open their own business. And you did.

---

girl talk

Shannon Davis
Founder, beyondmotherhood.com

After spending years in technology, staffing, and project management, Shannon Davis opted out to raise her two children. She loved being there for her children but wasn't entirely satisfied with her life and felt like she had more to offer. Then Shannon had her very own lightbulb moment. What about creating a business for women just like herself—smart, energetic, passionate moms who want or need more time for their families? Beyondmotherhood.com was soon born, and today it offers an on-line community, coaching, and niche job postings for moms.

As a mother, was becoming an entrepreneur a hard decision to make?

Actually it wasn't—for a couple reasons. One, I was doing something that was going to make me and many other moms happy, which in turn would make my family happy. Two, I was a choosing to create a business that would enable me to be there as a mother and as a businesswoman.

What do you find most challenging about balancing being a mom and an entrepreneur?

Realizing that no two days will be the same. Some days my business needs me more and sometimes my children do; the important thing is to not beat myself up and let others dictate what I "should" or "should not" be doing. Everyone's definition of balance is different; the key is to do what works for you, your family, and your business—and not sweat what other people are doing.

What is the best part about being a mom and an entrepreneur?

I love that my children (Maddy, age nine, and Alec, age six) are learning about entrepreneurship at such a young age. I love that they are seeing that Mommy can be there for them and also run a business.

Do you have advice for women thinking about starting their own businesses?

1. Think about *why* you want to do this. It will help you stay on track. My purpose was to have a career that was supportive of motherhood. This purpose has driven many decisions about how I've grown the business.

2. Be passionate about your idea.

3. Learn from others who have grown their own company, and interview successful people in all industries. There are so many lessons to be learned from just a brief interview. There's no reason to reinvent the wheel.

4. Don't let others pull you down. I always say it seems as soon as a budding entrepreneur mentions their idea for a new product or service, someone is quick to jump on them and say "somebody is already doing that!" No one ever says that to an attorney, doctor, or accountant when they decide to open up a practice down the street or even the hall from another attorney, doctor, or accountant. There is enough room on the playground for us all!

Do you have advice for women thinking about going after angel investors?

If you have people in your network who have received an angel investment, ask them for a referral. Don't limit yourself to investors in your city or state. Check out Springboard Enterprises (*www.springboardenterprises.org*) and Make Mine a Million (*www.makemineamillion.org*); they both provide great information and opportunities for female entrepreneurs.

How did you overcome your fears? Do you have tips to share with our readers?

I think that it starts with taking one hundred percent responsibility for your life, and you have to stop making excuses. I would be lying if I didn't say I still have fears, we all do; it's just now I don't let them paralyze me. The key is to acknowledge them, why you have them, and what you can do to push through them. A good exercise to do is to ask, "what is the worst thing that could happen if I do X?" and, "what is the best thing that could happen if I do X?" If you take no action, you stay where you are and keep getting what you're getting. If you want to grow and follow your passion, you're going to have to face your fears and push through them. Once you do, you will feel a sense of accomplishment that will carry you through your next fear. Each time it will get easier and easier.

Did you ever struggle with feeling too young or inexperienced to be running your own business?

I think it is normal to have moments when you feel insecure. The key is to push through them. The way to address these feelings is to surround yourself with people that are skilled in the areas you want to learn. They will get you up to speed much quicker than if you try to do it on your own. I remind myself that the talent is within me and that sometimes it just takes a little help pulling it out.

What do you see as the benefits to running your own business?

- Flexibility

- No two days are the same

- Developing new skills every day

- Becoming a great role model for my children

- Forcing myself to leave my comfort zone and explore new opportunities

Do you have any tips for keeping your family supportive of your business?

You need them to buy in from the beginning. If your husband or partner is not on board, it is going to create a rift between you and ultimately affect the success of your business. You need to sit down with your children and put their fears at ease, and you also need to continue checking in with them on a regular basis. Ask if they want to be involved (helping with mailings, events, packing for business trips, etc.). Schedule a regular date night with your husband or partner where you don't talk about your business (as entrepreneurs, our business often creeps into every conversation). Thank your family on a regular basis, and let them know that you could not have done this without their support. Explain to them that the success of the business is a credit to them.

Appendix
Helpful Web Sites for Girls
Going into Business

The Business Plan

Biz Plan It, *www.bizplanit.com*

MarketResearch.com, *www.marketresearch.com*

SCORE: Counselors to America's Small Business, *www.score.org*

Support and General Information

American Business Women's Association, *www.abwa.org*

Association for Enterprise Opportunity, *www.microenterpriseworks.org*

Catalyst (nonprofit research and advisory organization), *www.catalyst.org*

Center for Women's Business Research, *www.nfwbo.org*

Digital Women, *www.digital-women.com*

Entrepreneur.com, *www.entrepreneur.com*

National Association of Women Business Owners, *www.nawbo.org*

National Women's Business Council, *www.nwbc.gov*

Online Women's Business Center (Office of Women's Business Ownership, SBA), *www.onlinewbc.gov*

U.S. Small Business Administration, *www.sba.gov*

WomanOwned.com, *www.womanowned.com*

Franchises

Franchise Works.com, *www.franchiseworks.com*

Franchise Update, *www.franchise-update.com*

Funding

Springboard Enterprises, *www.springboardenterprises.org*

Taxes

Internal Revenue Service, *www.irs.gov*

Employees

Americans with Disabilities Act, *www.ada.gov*

U.S. Department of Labor, *www.dol.gov*

U.S. Equal Employment Opportunity Commission, *www.eeoc.gov*

Insurance

American Council of Life Insurers, *www.acli.com*

Cobra, *www.cobrahealth.com*

Insurance.com, *www.insurance.com*

On-line Resources

Online Women's Business Center, *www.onlinewbc.gov*

My Own Business, *www.myownbusiness.com*

Center For Business Planning, *www.businessplans.org*

Women's Business Center, *www.womenbiz.org*

Women-Owned Businesses, *www.business.gov/start/woman-owned/*

Women's Business Enterprise National Council, *www.wbenc.org*

BPW (Business and Professional Women's Foundation), *www.bpwusa.org*

Legalzoom, *www.legalzoom.com*

Inc., *www.inc.com*

Women Entrepreneur, *www.womenentrepreneur.com*

Women Entrepreneur Inc., *www.we-inc.org*

Ladies Who Launch, *www.ladieswholaunch.com*

Forum for Women Entrepreneurs and Executives, *www.fwe.org*

The International Alliance for Women, *www.tiaw.org*

Index

accountants, 56–59
  accounting software, 58, 61, 63
  and bookkeeping, 56, 57, 58, 61
  and business failures, 238
  and business plans, 92
  and employees, 134, 160–61
  and personal finances, 63
  and role of the business owner, 7
  and sole proprietorships, 53
  and taxes, 57, 59, 61
Active Capital, 72
Adams, Jody, 8, 233, 238
Adams, Nancy L., 55–56
advertising, 45, 106, 121–25, 171–72
Advertising Age web site, 171
Alford, Jeffrey, 32
American Recovery and Reinvestment
  Act of 2009 (Recovery Act), 68
Amy's Kitchen, 102
angel investors, 69, 72, 76, 242
apartment number 9, 42–43, 44–45
Apartment Therapy Media, 219–22
apologizing, 239
Apple, 103
Arieff, Adrienne, 4, 5
articles, writing, 127
assistance, ability to ask for, 10
attitude, 158
attorneys, 40, 50–52, 160, 238

auto insurance, 75, 78
award programs, 127

babysitters, 34
backups of data, 195
banks, 66–67
banner ads, 110, 122
benefits, 134
Berliner, Rachel, 102
birthdays, 225–26
BlackBerry phone services, 191
Blessing, Amy, 42–43, 44–45
Blessing, Sarah, 42–43, 44–45
blogging, 107
board of directors, 90, 127
bookkeeping and bookkeepers
  communication with, 61
  and payroll taxes, 60
  role of bookkeepers, 56
  and role of the business owner, 7,
    62
  software for, 58, 61, 63, 199
boredom, 4, 230
boss, being the. *See* employees
Boyer, Pat, 39–40
brainstorming sessions, 206–8
branding, 72
breaks, 34, 230
bridal and baby showers, 226

brochures, 106
budgets, 63–65, 72
burnout, 232
business cards, 106, 110
businesses, buying, 39–41
business plans, 83–93
    about, 83–84
    company description, 89
    executive summary, 85–87
    financials, 91–92
    funding request, 91
    market analysis, 87–89
    marketing and sales strategies,
        90–91
    organization and management, 89–90
    resources for, 84, 245
    service or product line, 91
Business Week web site, 171
business writing, 205–22
    brainstorming sessions, 206–8
    business letters, 208–10
    contracts, 215
    new-business proposals, 210–12
    presentations, 213–15
    proofreading pitfalls, 217–18
    RFP ("Request for Proposal")
        documents, 210–13
    TBNT ("Thanks but No Thanks")
        letters, 211
buying an existing business or franchise,
    39–41

calendar, 154
capital requirements, 29, 65–70
car insurance, 75, 78
Castiglia, Julie, 80–82
casualty insurance, 75
C corporations, 54
Center for Women's Business Research,
    20
Chanel, 103
character traits of successful
    entrepreneurs, 9–10
chick flicks for entrepreneurial
    inspiration, 20–23
children, 47, 235, 243
clothing choices, 165–66
COBRA (Consolidated Omnibus
    Budget Reconciliation Act), 74
commitments, keeping, 233
committee work, 127
communication, 233–34

competition
    and advertising, 122
    analysis of, 88
    and business plans, 88
    competitive personalities, 10
    competitive pricing, 74, 92
    cultivation of, 238
    and market research, 31, 43
    and public relations agencies, 114
    web sites of, 108
complaints and criticisms, 180
comp time, 151
computer consultants, 192, 193–95
computers, 192–93, 195–200
conference calls, 179
conferences, 127
confidence, 9, 238, 239
confrontations, 6, 25, 81, 180, 182–84
congratulatory notes, 226
consultants, 62. *See also* accountants;
        attorneys; bookkeepers
contact management software, 199–200
contracts, 215
control, 239–40
conversational skills, 231
Cornwell, Melinda, 166
corporate culture, 133
corporate identity, 102–5, 108
corporations, 54–55
county permits, 79
creativity, 29
credit cards, 66
current events, 231
customers and clients
    and advertising, 121–22
    and business meetings, 166–69
    and business plans, 87, 88, 90–91
    confrontations with, 183–84
    dependence on, 6–7
    drinks with, 172
    and e-mail, 125
    as friends, 229
    and market research, 42–43
    meals with, 172–74
    and networking, 62
    purchasing cycle of, 88
    and sales strategies, 90–91
    and target demographics, 73

Davis, Shannon, 240–43
debt financing, 66–69
decorating offices, 38

delivery services, 159
dental insurance, 146
Deregowski, Lynn, 23–27
diplomacy, 9
disability insurance, 76
discretion, 34
distractions, 34
domain names, 101–2, 194
dot-com boom, 69
dressing for success, 165–66, 177
drinks with clients, 172
DSL (digital subscriber lines), 197
DuBose, Carol, 135, 141, 151
Duffy, Laurice, 45–48
Duguid, Naomi, 31–32

e-commerce, 109. *See also* web sites
ego, 62, 235
e-mail
    confrontations through, 184
    and customer contact, 125
    etiquette in, 180
    personal e-mail, 159
    and professionalism, 34, 179
    protecting yourself in, 181–82
    and public relations agencies, 117
    responding to, 158–59
    and web sites, 110, 125
emotional boundaries, 227–28
employees, 133–63
    benefits, 134
    building loyalty, 151
    and business plans, 86
    and buying an existing business,
        40–41
    challenges related to, 47–48
    confrontations with, 183
    and corporate culture, 133
    employee manuals, 144–48, 150–51
    expense of, 134
    firing, 155–58
    as friends, 229
    hiring, 135–42, 160–61
    legal and financial considerations,
        160–61
    management of, 151–55
    resources for, 246
    retirement plans, 148–50
    setting an example for, 142–44
    as source of stress, 6
    temporary employees ("temps"), 135
    wages, 135, 145, 150, 151

employer identification number (EIN),
    59
employment agencies, 136
Entrepreneur.com, 170
Entrepreneur's annual Franchise 500, 41
equity financing, 69–70
etiquette, 179–82
executive search firms, 136
expansion, 38, 231
experience in the industry, 32–33
external hard drives, 195

Facebook, 107, 128, 136, 172
failure, 237–38
Fair Labor Standards Act of 1938
    (FLSA), 145, 146, 150
Family and Medical Leave Act (FMLA),
    147 .
family matters, 13, 235–36, 243
fear, 242
Febbroriello, Courtney, 32
feedback, 153
female musicians, 93–94
filing, 159
films for entrepreneurial inspiration,
    20–23
finances
    budgets, 63–65, 72
    and business plans, 91–92
    capital requirements, 29, 65–70, 246
    debt, 19, 66–69
    and employees, 143
    equity financing, 66, 69–70
    income, 11, 76
    and income fluctuation, 11, 19
    monthly expenses, 16–17
    personal finances, 16–19, 63
    preoccupation with, 7
    profits, 43, 72, 73
    saving money, 19
    and traits of successful entrepreneurs,
        29
fire department permits, 79
firewalls, 196–97
first impressions, 165
flexibility, 10
Flexible Executives, 136–37
Forman, Nancy, 57, 58, 67, 106, 236
401(k) plans, 149
franchises, 39–41, 246
freelancing and freelancers, 30, 76, 135
friends, 141, 142, 143, 228, 231

Gichon, Galia, 17–18, 57, 62
gifts, 224–26
Gillingham-Ryan, Maxwell, 219
Gillingham-Ryan, Sara Kate, 219–22
goals and goal setting, 32, 95–96
GoldMine contact management
    software, 199–200
gossip, 181
government, 68–69
grammar skills, 218
graphic designers, 105
growth, preparing for, 101

Haber, Elaine, 58, 59, 61, 62, 67, 237
hair styles, 166
Harris, Paula, 129
health insurance, 74–75, 146
health permits, 78
Herrington, Carrie, 66, 67, 100–101
hobbies, 31–32, 230
holidays, 146, 225
home-business insurance, 77
Huffington Post web site, 171

Inc.com, 171
income, 11, 76
incorporated business structures, 54–55
independence, 8, 29
industries, changing, 31
insecurity, 242–43
instincts, 223
insurance, 74–78, 146, 246
Internal Revenue Service (IRS), 59,
    147–48
Internet
    connectivity to, 194, 197–99
    dot-com boom, 69
    and employment listings, 138
    and home office, 35
    See also web sites
Internet telephony, 190
interview questions, 139–40
investors and business plans, 87, 91
iPhone, 191
IP telephony, 190
IRAs (individual retirement accounts),
    149–50
IT (information technologies)
    consultants, 192, 193–95
iTelephony, 190

jury duty, 146

Katzen, Anita, 30
Keepin, Betty, 165, 174
Kincaid, Betty A., 35
Kirshenbaum, Susan, 111, 121, 124
Kisielewska, Larissa, 201–4
The Kitchn blog, 219–22

landlines, 188
Lauren, Ralph, 73
layoffs, 156
leadership, 10, 127
learning, opportunities for, 8, 224, 230
leases, 40
Lee, Monica, 70–71
legal structures, 52–56, 90
letterhead, 106, 110
Levin, Carrie, 10, 13, 144, 152, 154
liability protection, 52, 54, 55–56, 75
libraries, 87
licenses and permits, 78–79, 89
life insurance, 76, 146
limitations, managing, 168–69
limited liability companies (LLCs),
    55–56
limited liability partnerships (LLPs),
    55–56
LinkedIn, 128, 136, 172
liquor licenses, 79
living expenses, 16–17
local area networks (LAN), 196
location of business, 43, 86–87, 107
logos, 102–5
lunch with clients, 172–74

Mac computers, 201–4
mailing supplies, 159
mail-merge programs, 117
Make Mine a Million, 242
makeup, 166
management, 89, 90, 151–55
mantras, 238–40
market analysis for business plans,
    87–89
marketing, 100–132
    about, 72, 105–6
    advertising, 45, 106, 121–25,
        171–72
    budget for, 106, 110, 121, 124
    and business plans, 90–91
    corporate identity, 102–5, 108
    logos, 102–5
    market research, 30, 41–43

naming your business, 100–103
promotions, 106, 110–11, 122
public relations, 106, 111–20
referral arrangements, 110
resources for, 171–72
during slow times, 236–37
and social networking, 106, 107,
    128–29, 172
speaking engagements, 106, 126,
    127, 177–79
special events and sponsorships, 128
target market, 73, 88
viral marketing, 128
See also web sites
markup, 73
Martin, Ti, 136, 141, 151, 154
Maxwell, Jenny, 23–27
McWillie, Betty, 28, 29
meals, 172–74, 175
media coverage, 110, 111–18
meetings, 152–53, 166–67
mentors and mentoring, 127, 226–27
merchandising, 43
Microloan Program, 69
Microsoft Business Plan template, 92
Microsoft FrontPage, 108
Microsoft Outlook, 117
mission statements, 86
mistakes, acknowledging, 184, 239
mobile phones, 188
money purchase retirement plans,
    148–49
monthly expenses, 16–17
moonlighting, 30
movies for entrepreneurial inspiration,
    20–23
music, 93–94
Mussaffi, Susan, 161

naming your business, 100–103
national conferences, 127
National Women's Business Council, 84
negativity, 228
neighbors, 141
net income, 73
network, computer, 194, 196–99
networking, 30–31, 62, 73, 106, 110,
    126
new-business proposals, 210–12
newspapers, 138, 232
Newsweek web site, 170
Nike, 103

Norton, Sarilee, 213
notepaper, 224
Nudo, 112–13

Obama administration, 67, 68
Oberhelman, Susi, 102
O'Brien, Deirdre, 50, 51, 52–53, 54, 63
O'Conner, Patricia T., 218
Office of Women's Business Ownership,
    227
offices, 33–39
    decorating, 38
    home offices, 33–35
    office duties, 158
    office hours, 145
    renting offices, 35–39
    supplies for, 159
one-woman operations, 134
Oprah web site, 171
organizational skills, 9, 158–59
overtime pay, 150

partners and partnerships, 25, 53–54,
    55–56, 228, 233–35
part-time entrepreneurship, 20
part-time jobs, 31
Paterson, Tara, 110, 226, 231, 235
Paul, Martine, 58
payday, 145
payroll companies, 148
payroll taxes, 57, 60, 134
PC computers, 201–4
Pennington, Jamie, 136–37
performance reviews, 150–51
permits and licenses, 78–79, 89
personal days, 146
personal finances, 16–19, 63
personal life, 232
phones and phone services, 34, 37, 179,
    188–91
pitch letters, 209–10
planning skills, 9
positive people, 99
PowerPoint presentations, 213–14
preparedness for launching a business,
    14–15, 224
Prequalification Pilot Loan Program,
    68–69
presentations, 177–79, 213–15
press clips and releases, 115, 117–20.
    See also public relations
pretax income, 73

pricing, 43, 74, 92, 169
pride, 240
products, 73–74, 87, 91, 110–11
professionalism, 164–86
   and business travel, 174–77
   and drinks with clients, 172
   and e-mail, 34, 179
   and etiquette, 179
   and meals with clients, 172–74
   and new-business meetings, 166–69
   and personal style, 165–66
   and presentations, 177–79
professional organizations, 30–31,
   126–27
profits, 43, 72, 73
profit-sharing plans, 149
promotions, 106, 110–11, 122
proofreading pitfalls, 217–18
property insurance, 75
public relations, 106, 111–20
public speaking, 126, 127, 177–79
purchasing cycles, 88

QuickBooks and Quicken software, 58,
   60, 199

real estate agents, 35–36
receipts, 58–59, 175
record keeping and filing, 58–59
reenergizing yourself, 229–31
referral arrangements, 110
registration of companies, 59
reimbursable expenses, 150
"Request for Proposal" (RFP)
   documents, 210–13
research, 223–24
respect, 7
responsibility, 144, 151, 242
retail stores, 44–45
retirement plans, 147–48
risk taking, 10
Rotheiser, Brenda, 220
routers, 196–97
Ryan, Rebecca, 215–17

Sack, Celia, 129–32
sales strategies, 90–91
Saperstan, Joan, 236
SBALowDoc Loan Program, 69
schedules and time management, 4, 5,
   33, 154
Schwalbe, Will, 182

SCORE: Counselors to America's Small
   Business, 92, 93
S corporations, 55
security, 37
SEPs (Simplified Employee Pension
   plans), 149–50
services, 73–74, 87, 91, 110–11
7 (a) Loan Guaranty Program, 68
Shipley, David, 182
sick days, 146
significant others and spouses, 235, 243
sign permits, 79
SIMPLE (Savings Incentive Match Plan
   for Employees) IRAs, 149–50
single member LLCs (SMLLCs), 56
Skype, 188, 190
sleep, importance of, 33, 175
slow times, 236–37
Small Business Administration (SBA),
   68, 93
Smart Money web site, 171
smartprice.com, 190
social networking
   and employee recruitment, 136, 172
   guidelines for using, 128–29
   and marketing, 106, 107, 128–29,
   172
Society for Human Resource
   Management, 135
software, 199
sole proprietorships, 53, 69, 76, 149
speaking engagements, 106, 126, 127,
   177–79
special events and sponsorships, 106,
   128
spell-check programs, 118, 217
spiritual well-being, 229
spouses and significant others, 235, 243
Springboard Enterprise, 70–71, 242
staff. *See* employees
Starbucks, 103
state licenses, 79
storage space, 38–39
strategic thinking, 29
stress management, 6, 25, 81, 200–201
style, personal, 165–66
success in business, 223–24
Sutton, Judith, 217

Target, 103
target market, 73, 88
taxes, 59–60

and accountants and bookkeepers, 57, 59, 61
and business travel, 175
and incorporation, 52–53, 54–55
and limited liability companies, 56
payroll taxes, 57, 60, 134
quarterly payments, 53
resources for, 246
responsibility for, 7, 57
and sole proprietorships, 53
technology, 187–204
computers and Internet access, 192–200 (*see also* Internet; web sites)
phone lines and services, 34, 37, 188–91
temporary employees ("temps"), 135
thank-you cards and gifts, 224–25
time management, 158–59
Time web site, 170
Toastmasters International, 178
to-do lists, 158
Tooker, Sylvia, 109
trade publications, 138
traits of successful entrepreneurs, 9–10, 29
travel, 174–77
Treco-Jones, Sherry, 105–6, 114–15, 236–37
Twitter, 107, 128, 172

U.S. Chamber of Commerce, 69
U.S. Department of Labor, 144, 146

vacation time, 145–46, 232
values, 86

Vasquez, Frank, 194–95
venture capital firms, 69–71, 76
viral marketing, 128
voice mail, 188
Voice Over IP (VoIP), 188, 190, 191

Wall Street Journal web site, 172
wardrobe choices, 165–66
web sites, 106–10
and banner ads, 110, 122
design of, 107–9
and domain names, 101–2, 194
and e-commerce, 109
and e-mail, 110, 125
and hosting services, 109
and market research, 43
and naming your business, 100, 101
and search engines, 109
ten web sites and blogs to follow, 170
and web designers, 102, 108, 125
and web presence, 194
See also Internet
Winfrey, Oprah, 171
Wolfer, Chris, 94–99, 182
women-owned businesses, statistics on, 20
Women's Business Center, 83, 84, 85, 87, 92, 95
workday, length of, 8
workers' compensation, 76, 78
work habits, 10, 142–44

Yellow Pages, 122
Yorio, Sharyn, 126

zoning regulations, 40